The Miracle

of Dialogue

By the Author:

Man's Need and God's Action

The Creative Years

Herein Is Love

REUEL L. HOWE

The
Miracle
of
Dialogue

A Crossroad Book

THE SEABURY PRESS · NEW YORK

ACKNOWLEDGMENTS

Grateful acknowledgment is made to the following publishers and authors for permission to quote from the copyrighted titles listed:

Macmillan Company and the Beacon Press—Martin Buber, *Between Man and Man.*

The University of Chicago Press—Maurice S. Friedman, *Martin Buber: the Life of Dialogue.*

Twenty-second Printing

© 1963 by The Seabury Press, Incorporated

Library of Congress Catalog Card Number: 62-17080

ISBN: 0-8164-2047-5

Design by Lewis F. White

Printed in the United States of America

To my students

WHO IN DIALOGUE BECOME

MY TEACHERS

Contents

Preface

THE first formal presentation of the subject matter of this book was made when I gave the Kellogg Lectures, 1961, to the faculty, students, alumni, and guests of the Episcopal Theological School, Cambridge, Massachusetts. Those lectures have now been revised and expanded, with the end in view of making them available and of interest to anyone who is concerned with communication. All of us, in one way or another, are trying to communicate with ("get into significant touch with") someone, and all of us, to some degree, are baffled by the failure of our attempts. Seminars with laymen and clergymen, at the Institute for Advanced Pastoral Studies, have not only revealed to me the nature and extent of this frustration but have given me, I believe, some clues to the answers of the problem.

vii

The insights of this book come out of years of dialogue with my students, and to them I dedicate it. They have been, and are, theological students, clergymen, and laymen who, having been invited to be active rather than passive participants in learning, discovered the joy of doing their own thinking in relation to the thinking of others, and also found that the truth emerging from dialogue, when embodied in men and communities, is empowered for responsible action. With them I, too, experienced what I am writing about here. I want them to know that they have helped me prepare this book.

Also, I must acknowledge my indebtedness to the writings of Martin Buber, especially his essay on "Education" in *Between Man and Man* (Beacon Press), and to Maurice S. Friedman's study *Martin Buber: the Life of Dialogue* (University of Chicago Press).

I offer this little volume with the hope that it will call forth courage for a life of dialogue through which the miracles of reconciliation may be accomplished.

REUEL L. HOWE

Bloomfield Hills, Michigan
September 1, 1962

1 The Importance of Dialogue

EVERY man is a potential adversary, even those whom we love. Only through dialogue are we saved from this enmity toward one another. Dialogue is to love, what blood is to the body. When the flow of blood stops, the body dies. When dialogue stops, love dies and resentment and hate are born. But dialogue can restore a dead relationship. Indeed, this is the miracle of dialogue: it can bring relationship into being, and it can bring into being once again a relationship that has died.

There is only one qualification to these claims for dialogue: it must be mutual and proceed from both sides, and the parties to it must persist relentlessly. The word of dialogue may be spoken by one side but evaded or ignored by the other, in which case the promise may not be fulfilled. There is risk in speaking the dialogical word—that is, in entering into dialogue—but when two persons undertake it and accept their fear of doing so, the miracle-working power of dialogue may be released.

If the claims we are making here for dialogue are a cause for surprise to the reader, the reason may be that dialogue has been equated too exclusively with the conversational parts of a play. We think of it differently—as the serious address and response between two or more persons, in which the being and truth of each is confronted by the being and truth of the other. Dialogue, therefore, is not easy and comfortable to achieve, a fact which may explain why it occurs so rarely. And its rare occurrence accounts for the frequent absence of its benefits in our communication with one another.

To say that communication is important to human life is to be trite, but that bit of triteness witnesses to an invariable truth: communication means life or death to persons. A study of the nature of communication is needed in this day of mass communication. On a colossal scale never known before and with technical aids that surpass the wildest imaginings of yesterday's science fiction, man can bombard his fellow man's mind, feelings, and will with a subtleness and effectiveness that is frightening. Books like *The Hidden Persuaders* by Vance Packard describe how man becomes the victim of communication rather than communication being a means by which he finds himself in his relation with other men in a community of mutual criticism and helpfulness.

Both the individual and society derive their basic meaning from the relations that exist between man and man. At the moment of birth the individual comes into personal being in response to his being met by his mother and father and all the others who care for him in all the concreteness of his need. And out of that same meeting the family community is born. Many people think that the individual as a social being derives from a "given" social nature of man; others hold that society and interpersonal relations are the sum of individual lives. Neither of these views recognizes that upon which both depend, namely, the interaction between the individual and his personal environment. Recently a group of ministers was told that until the Church becomes a community, it will not be able to communicate adequately. Left unanswered was the question: How does the Church or any other group of people become a community? And the answer is simple: it becomes a community when as persons, the members enter into dialogue with one another and assume responsibility for their common life. Without this dialogue individuals and society are abstractions. It is through dialogue that man accomplishes the miracle of personhood and community.

There are many illustrations of the importance of dialogue. Earlier, reference was made to the infant's becoming a person in response to the meeting between him and his family. From the very beginning of the individual's life it is communication that guarantees its continuation. While dependent on food and care, the newborn infant also needs the communication that is implicit in them and conveyed in the way they are given. Mother feeds and bathes, cuddles and sings to her baby, and through this activity the infant receives the message that she loves him and wants him. This message also means to him that he is loved and therefore lovable, accepted and therefore acceptable. Or, if his mother is hostile and irritable and expresses her resentment in neglect and roughness, he receives the contrary message that she regards him as a nuisance, which conveys to him that he is unloved and unlovable, unaccepted and unacceptable. In the first instance, the message of love and care is life-giving and nurturing; in the second, the message is alienating and destructive. And this is true for mother as well as for child, because in loving and serving her child the mother is giving herself, making herself available as a person to him. For the act of loving another gives life to the lover as well as to the one loved, and to speak the word of love is to be loved as well as to love.

The infant participates in this dialogue, too. He cries, waves his arms, kicks his legs, and in other non-verbal ways asks his questions and makes his positive and negative comments about his life. The response of his world, made to him by his mother and those around him, influences quite decisively his future capacity for communication. If his initial communications are accepted, not necessarily approved,* he will grow in his capacity to speak; if they are not, he will become inhibited, resentful, and defensive, which in turn may only increase his mother's destructive communication. Sometimes the communication between them makes both sad and listless, and at other times glad and alive.

The relation between a man and a woman also can re-

---

* Acceptance and approval are not the same. Many mistakenly think that to accept a person one must approve or at least not show disapproval of what he is doing. Judgment is always implicit and sometimes explicit in acceptance. Approval of behavior can sometimes mean the rejection of the individual as a responsible person.

veal how indispensable is the life of dialogue. In addition to their differences as man and woman, there are other multifaceted differences between them. Some event in which each has participated has brought them together, such as a meeting of eyes or the recognition in a discussion that they share the same opinion or attitude. In this kind of event the dialogue begins. Each then undertakes to seek and explore the other. It is important to know who the other truly is, and through dialogue that employs both the language of relationship and the language of words to seek to know life through the other. Love is born out of this dialogue in which there is both the intimacy of what these two people share in common and the distance of the unplumbed mystery of each. The emergence of this mutual awareness in the relationship reveals an important distinction between monological and dialogical love. Monological love enjoys only self-centeredly the feelings of a relationship. The lover exploits the beloved for the sake of the emotional dividend to be had. In contrast, dialogical love is outgoing. The lover turns to the beloved not to enjoy her selfishly but to serve her, to know her, and through her to be. Correspondingly, the beloved seeks the lover not to enjoy him for herself but to serve him, to know him, and in knowing him and being known by him to find her own being. In dialogical love there is enjoyment of love, but since it is not exploitive, the enjoyment increases rather than diminishes the power to love.

Marriage is an ultimate commitment to this kind of human relationship, expressing the realization that to become a person one has to share in the being of another, and that one has to offer oneself as a person, in relation with whom the other may participate in the realization of his own being. The dialogue is in earnest. And every aspect of the relationship becomes a vehicle for it: verbal activity, living together, the assumption of responsibilities, sexual relations, and recreation. And this relationship will continue to be a living one so long as each keeps in communication with the other. Each must try to speak honestly out of his own conviction, discipline his subjective feelings, seek patiently to keep aware of the partner as another person, and try to keep open to the meaning of everything that happens in the relationship. Whenever either party begins to be more concerned for himself than for the other, when he uses the other as a thing for any purpose whatever, when he hides in defensive behavior, the marriage has become monological and broken. When this happens either or both of the partners may indignantly demand that the other repent and reform in the interest of a mended relationship. Healing of a marriage or any other relationship cannot occur when the partners see themselves as separate individuals with a right to demand services of each other. Healing can come only when one or the other is able to turn toward his partner, to accept the risk of giving himself in love, and to search himself for whatever reform may be necessary. A wife, for example, may be able to make this kind of gift, and yet have it fail to heal because her husband cannot accept her gift and give himself in return. But if he can, then the miracle will occur and the dead relationship will be called again into life.

The relationship between parents and children also calls for a practice of the principle of dialogue. How hard it is for parents to respect and trust the uniqueness and powers of their children! While there are those aspects of life in which parents must decide and act for them until such time as they are able to decide and act for themselves, children should always have the experience of being met as free persons in a trusting and responsible relationship. The need for this trust increases as the children grow older, and it becomes acute at adolescence when the transition from childhood to adulthood is taking place. Then it is imperative that young persons be allowed their freedoms, but equally imperative that they also have encounter with persons of conviction who, at the same time, respect their freedoms. Without this kind of relationship the individual simply flees from life, becomes passive and locked up within himself; or he may become a fighting person whose creativity is lost in the wastelands of his aggression. The importance of dialogue for this juncture of growth lies in the fact that it expresses mutual respect so that youth need neither repress creativity nor throw it away, and age need neither seek to dominate nor turn away from youth in frustration. In those instances where the young person has withdrawn from life or is in hostile combat with it, as in delinquency, dialogue may accomplish the miracle of bringing the young person back into a creative relation to life.

Dialogue is indispensable also in the search for truth and here, too, it is a worker of miracles. Unfortunately, many people hold and proclaim what they believe to be true in either an opinionated or defensive way. Religious people, for example, sometimes speak the truth they profess monologically, that is, they hold it exclusively and inwardly as if there was no possible relation between what they believe and what others believe, in spite of every indication that separately held truths are often complementary. The monological thinker runs the danger of being prejudiced, intolerant, bigoted, and a persecutor of those who differ from him. The dialogical thinker, on the other hand, is willing to speak out of his convictions to the holders of other convictions with genuine interest in them and with a sense of the possibilities between them.

Let us take, for example, a man who, as a student of human relations, is interested in the functioning of groups. At the moment he believes that the dynamics of a group are best understood by studying the individual and what happens to him as a member of the group. This student could hold this view of group process aggressively and defensively against all other theories; but in that case his view would remain unaffirmed, uncorrected, and without complement of or completion by other views. Instead, he turns from his "individual-centered" view of group process to the "group-centered" interpretation, with the honest desire to discover what group life looks like from that point of view. He thus brings his own theory into dialogue with another, and when he discovers that the two are complementary, his earlier understanding is broadened and deepened. He may also discover that he contributed something to the theory he examined. Then he learns of still another view, the "reality-centered" concept of group life, to which he now turns dialogically. Each of these views, when held separately and uncriticized or unmodified by the views of others, is inadequate for a complete interpretation of group life. In dialogue, however, these views mutually qualify and supplement each other and thus provide a comprehensive view that is more completely the truth than is any one of them by itself. When this comprehensive concept of group relations is now brought into dialogue with different theological insights into human relations, a yet more profound and inclusive view of group relations will emerge. Dialogue, therefore, produces miracles of discovery, opening to us the mysteries of life.

Another area in desperate need of dialogical spirit and action is that of politics. National parties are often pitted against each other solely in the interest of their own success and sometimes to the cost of the country they are professing to serve; and nations look toward themselves and not toward each other, thus threatening the welfare of the planet. Indeed, the human race stands in danger of being destroyed because of the deliberate effort of parties and nations to advance their own cause by falsifying the aims and character of their opponents. With this frequently goes an ignoring of one's own sin and responsibility, a representation of the self as being better than it is, and a sense of injury at the hands of the other, as if the fiction created about them was true. The abuse of dialogue has gone on so long that politicians find it difficult to break out of their monological fantasies and move toward a dialogical meeting. What is needed is the coming together of men of conviction from their respective camps who are willing to talk honestly with one another in the face of mutual criticism and loyalty to their own views. If these men would speak with one another not as pawns on a chessboard but as themselves in the sanctuary of truth, the sphere of public life would be transformed by the miracle of dialogue.

Still another area of life in which communication is indispensably important is industry and business. It is claimed by those within industry and by critics on the outside that mechanization and industrialization have a depersonalizing effect on people; that persons are reduced to things and made to serve the purposes of industry as if they were merely cogs of a machine. This is said to be true not only of the man who works in the shop or on the line but of the executive as well. To deny that these conditions are true is to deny available evidence.

There are, however, other factors that can serve to combat dehumanizing influences. Men in business are persons with capacity for personal relations which can be exercised in spite of the impersonal forces lined up against the personal. But the quality of dialogue has to be in those relations, and this means that each of the participants must hold in mind his fellow workers in their present and particular being and turn to them with the intention of establishing a mutual relation between himself and them. This possibility was acknowledged by the businessman who admitted that he made it a part of his business enterprise to keep his competitor in focus as a person by being interested in him and in his interests, and by regarding him as one deserving the same respect he wanted for himself. The ordinary man can, and at times does, break through "from the status of the dully-tempered disagreeableness, obstinacy and contrariness in which he lives" into a life of personal fulfillment by acts of self-giving. Martin Buber states it:

> No factory and no office is so abandoned by creation that a creative glance could not fly up from one working-place to another, from desk to desk, a sober and brotherly glance which guarantees the reality of creation which is happening—*quantum satis*. And nothing is so valuable a service of dialogue between God and

man as such an unsentimental and unreserved exchange of glances between two men in an alien place.

It is also possible for a leader of business to fill his business with dialogue by meeting the men with whom he works as persons. Even when he cannot meet them directly, he can be 'inwardly aware, with a latent and disciplined fantasy, of the multitude of persons,' so that when one of them does step before him as an individual, he can meet him 'not as a number with a human mask but as a person.' *

While the personal seems to be threatened by the intricacy and massiveness of modern industrial enterprise, it must be remembered that this enterprise was and is being built by creative persons and can only be maintained by them. No better illustration of this can be found than in the radical transformations that occur in business organizations when the leadership passes from one person to another. The question then, is: Will machines and organizations created by man destroy him, or will he control and use them for creative purposes?

This question will be answered in part by the relationships achieved in business—between labor and management, for example. Here is an area of life which needs to be touched by the transforming power of dialogue. In the midst of a labor dispute or the working out of a contract agreement, when the two parties are meeting across the table, the question needs to be asked: Is the discussion monologue or dialogue? If it is competitive only and moti-

* Maurice S. Friedman, *Martin Buber* (University of Chicago Press, 1955), p. 88. (Now a Harper Torchbook.)

vated by concern of each side for itself alone, then it is monologue. If, on the other hand, the discussion is informed by
each party's honest representation of itself and its aims *and*
a genuine "seeing the other" or "experiencing the other side"
of the dispute, true dialogue will occur out of which creative
settlement may more likely appear. When a condition of
stalemate is followed by a settlement it means that the
parties finally abandoned an earlier determination to see the
situation only from their own point of view and began to
look at it also from the side of their opponents. The discussion changed from monologue to dialogue, thus making a
settlement possible.

The separation between the world and the Church also
calls for the ministry of dialogue. The Church sometimes
withdraws from the world, refuses to communicate with it,
and treats it as an enemy rather than as the place of its life
and mission. An all too prevailing attitude among church
people is that the Church has much to say to the world but
that the world has nothing to say that the Church should
hear. When the Church is preoccupied with its own concerns and oblivious to the world, its communication becomes
monological and not equal to the task of telling men the
Good News. The true concern of religion is not religion, but
life. The gift of God in Christ is not for the Church but for
all men, and the Church is sent not to itself but to the world.

The responsibility of the Church is to speak dialogically
with each generation and thus meet the needs of men. And
the Church's own need for renewal is met through such dialogue. The exchange between the Church and the world,
if it is genuine, must have mutual effect. A word spoken in

isolation cannot have the same meaning as the same word spoken in relation. Likewise, the Word of God is best understood when it is spoken in relation to the word of man for whom it was given. Those who proclaim that Word, therefore, have as much responsibility to understand the word of man as they do the Word of God in order that they may help men to recognize and accept their need of God's Word. The vitality of religious teaching is dependent in part upon its awareness and response to the meanings and questions of human life. The word *tradition* means "from hand to hand." Religious tradition becomes dead and sterile when it passes through generations without real encounter with them. When there is dialogue between truth and life, the tradition grows, accumulates understanding and skill, and becomes equal to the challenges of each new age. The concepts of religion, therefore, have to be kept in dialogue with man and confirmed in his life. We have the same Bible that men had 1500 years ago, but our understanding of it and its power to illumine human life is much greater than at that time as a result of the dialogue between biblical study and scientific, literary, psychological, and anthropological studies.

The most important thing about this dialogue between the Church and the world is that God acts in and through it to influence both the Church and the world and to judge, purify, and transform both. The Church originated from man's relation to God in Christ and its vitality is dependent upon the continuation of this God-man relation and not on conceptual formulations about the relation. The life of the world moves from one crucial relational event to another and can only be kept creative by finding its meaning in per-

sonal encounter through which God acts. The dialogue between religion and culture is necessary to both, and out of
it comes the miracle of re-creation for both.

Finally, the sphere of education calls for the applica-
tion of the principle of dialogue. Two views of education
compete for acceptance: (1) *transmission,* which seeks to
educate by funneling what needs to be known from the
teacher to the pupil; and (2) *induction,* which seeks to draw
forth from the student his creative powers in relation to his
interest in and need for the world around him. The authoritarian kind of education places emphasis on the content
of the curriculum, and the permissive theory emphasizes the
student and his freedom to learn. Each theory is inadequate
to the task of education. The authoritarian theory ignores
the student and what he brings to the educational encounter;
and the permissive theory ignores the disciplines necessary
to learning; and both ignore the significance and power of
the relationship between teacher and student upon which
the whole educational enterprise finally depends. The student must be free to explore and think, but he needs also to
be met by a teacher who embodies in himself the data and
meaning of the world and who trusts the student to respond
creatively when he presents it. The educator faces two temp-
tations: first, to interfere and force the student to learn and
respond by imposing his own opinion and attitudes on him,
so that he becomes either obedient or rebellious or a confused mixture of both; and second, in the name of freedom,
to leave the student without benefit of direction.

Some educators belittle and ignore the intellectual discipline; others neglect the significance of the relation between
the student and teacher. Actually, the two belong together.

That which is to be taught comes from man's relation with himself and his fellows and the world in which they live. The learning of these things, therefore, should not be abstracted from the relationship from which they come, to which they belong, and to which they must be re-related if learning is to produce in the learner appreciation and creative power. There must be dialogue between teacher and student, and between the meaning as formulated in theory out of men's past experience and meaning as it emerges out of their contemporary experience. The miracle of dialogue in education is the calling forth of persons who have found their own unique relation to truth and who serve that truth with creative expectancy.

We have now examined the importance of dialogue by looking at its role in several of life's important relationships. Where there is dialogue, there is communication. Yet attempts at communication often fail. Why, we must ask. What are the barriers to communication that keep dialogue from occurring and that dialogue must overcome?

2 The Barriers to Communication

To say that communication is a problem is to say nothing new, for men always have had to strive to make themselves understood. Each age, however, has its own peculiar communication problems; and our age, possessing as it does an amazing means for increasing, extending, and amplifying communication, confronts in the process both greater potential and greater frustration. While the mass media for communication have increased so that people today are bombarded with news and propaganda of all kinds, their understanding of and sensitivity to events and ideas seem to be decreasing. At a conference, recently, an educated, intelligent man complained that he read, heard, and saw so much that he was finding it impossible to sort this all out and come to any clear understanding that might serve as a firm basis for his decisions and actions.

Some Areas of Frustration

Every area of human life provides us with illustrations of the frustrations that men experience in their attempts to communicate. Parents' anxieties about their children often keep them from seeing their children as they are, and from hearing and responding to them. And children's preoccupations and their growing images of adults in general, and their parents in particular, make it difficult for them to hear and respond to their parents. At a recent meeting a mother said, "I never feel that my children hear what I am really saying. Their hearing seems to be influenced by what they expect me to say."

Marital relations reveal the same sense of frustration. Husbands and wives lose the power to share the meanings of their lives. Instead, accumulations of frustration and resentment produce alienation that makes it impossible for them to speak to one another in any language, whether that of words or of action. Something seems to block their ability to assume joint responsibility for the real curriculum of their relationship. "Our only communication," said one man, "is at the level of superficialities." A wife said, her voice strident with bitterness, "We piggy-back on the trivial."

Relations between churches is another area that reveals the difficulties of communication. Churches that really have much in common that should bind them together nevertheless find conversation for unity unbelievably difficult because of the differences that separate them. Here again, misconceptions of each other block both address and response. A

Baptist said of an Episcopalian, "I cannot hear you because of what I expect you to say."

And, too, people from different cultures are often predisposed not to hear and understand each other. Not until some representative of one or the other side breaks through in convincing and reassuring language is it possible for a mutual relationship between them to develop. An excellent illustration was Benny Goodman's visit to Russia, where his music spoke to many Russians, who, in turn, responded with such enthusiasm that feelings of kinship displaced the old feelings of suspicion and alienation.

A recent survey of a thousand ministers from various denominations and with widely different educational backgrounds showed that all of them designated communication as their primary concern. The chief source of their frustration was their sense of failing to open the lives of their people at any deep level to the meanings of the gospel. Laymen, from their side, see the failure of communication to lie in the fact that the preacher's sermon, for example, on the free gift of God's love is often heard by them simply as a new and harsher demand to be good. The preaching of "grace" is heard as a demand of "law."

Some Barriers That Block Meeting of Meaning

Why, we must ask, is communication so consistently frustrated? In answering this question let us examine, first, the communication between two individuals. Later, we can apply what we learn to communication between the individual and the group, and between groups.

As an aid to understanding the situation in communication and the barriers that make its accomplishment so difficult, we shall use Diagram A.

DIAGRAM A

THE COMMUNICATION PROBLEM

Types of Speakers and Hearers	Meaning Barriers	Types of Speakers and Hearers
Parents		Children
Wives	Language	Husbands
Students	Images	Teachers
Salesmen	Anxieties	Customers
Congregation	Defenses	Preacher
Labor	Purposes	Management
Whites		Negroes
Roman Catholics		Protestants
Church	↑ ↑ ↑ ↑ ↑	World
	ONTOLOGICAL NEEDS OF EVERY HUMAN BEING	

When we undertake to communicate with another, we address ourselves to him with the expectation that he will respond. We expect that the meanings we are trying to convey will activate certain meanings in him out of which he will reply, and that each will continue in a mutual and reciprocal exchange of meanings until some purpose has been accomplished. Any participant listed in either outer column of Diagram A may initiate the conversation. The speaker and the one spoken to, however, will bring to it meanings that are both a resource for and barrier to communication. For we can assume without danger of error that people always bring meaning to every encounter. We may not be aware of it and we may not recognize the meaning they bring; or, the meanings may be unacceptable so that we may find it necessary to reject them. Sometimes, we say that a situation does not have meaning or that a person does not make sense. Fundamentally, these observations are always wrong. There is never a situation that is without some meaning, and our task is not to dismiss it as meaningless but to open our eyes and ears and look for the meaning that lies behind what appears to have none. When a situation seems to be without meaning, all we are justified in saying is that we cannot see the meaning that is there.

A woman, for example, said of her husband, "Your way of life doesn't make sense." In private conversation the man himself also said that his life didn't make sense. When he was asked why he worked so hard and was busy in so many community activities, he replied, "If I didn't do what I'm doing, I would lose my self-respect." We now observe that his way of life, far from being senseless, is his way of trying to find his worth. At this point we may wish to help him evaluate and decide whether his attempts at self-justification are fulfilling his hopes for himself. Our insight, then, into the meaning of his behavior opens a door to relationship with him and reveals the creative possibilities in continuing conversation with him. On the other hand, had we merely concluded that his life was senseless, further communication with him would have held little promise of being fruitful. In analyzing the process of communication, therefore, one of our first conclusions is that in every encounter between man and man each person brings out of his life meanings that are available for communication.

We are now ready to define communication, to identify the relation in which it takes place. It occurs whenever there is a meeting of meaning between two or more persons. There was no meeting of meaning between the over-busy husband and his wife. Turning to the diagram again, we know that in her concern she tried many times to reach him. Although she loved him, she was alienated by his preoccupation with other interests. In telling him that she did not see any sense in what he was doing, she missed the meaning of his activities. He, in turn, was alienated by her rejection of him so that he could neither respond to her concern nor express his own. We now have a typical breakdown of communication with the usual stalemate in relationship, the cause being the failure of both parties to be open to the meanings of the "other side." The wife's message of love bearing her concern hit a meaning barrier and thus, short of the mark and unfulfilled, returned to her, instead of reaching her husband as she had hoped. And the husband's message of self-concern, expressed through his way of life, also hit a meaning barrier and thus, short of the mark and unfulfilled, returned to him, instead of reaching his wife and her understanding. Each is now walled off from the other, and any exchange that goes on between them is superficial and unable to illumine the deep real concerns of each.

A barrier to communication is something that keeps meanings from meeting. Meaning barriers exist between all people, making communication much more difficult than most people seem to realize. It is false to assume that if one can talk, he can communicate. Because so much of our education misleads people into thinking that communication is easier than it is, they become discouraged and give up when they run into difficulty. Because they do not understand the nature of the problem, they do not know what to do. The wonder is not that communication is as difficult as it is, but that it occurs as much as it does. Education, training for leadership, preparation for marriage and parenthood, should at least give people an understanding of the nature of communication, how it occurs, and how they may carry out their responsibility for it. Many leaders, educators, and ministers —not to mention others—however, go into their work without any adequate understanding of the nature of communication or of the barriers that have to be broken through in communication; instead, they have the mistaken idea that the mere desire to say something is enough. Any process of education or training that sends men to the task of communication without some rudimentary understanding of it or with false expectations for it is cruel and irresponsible and only serves to condemn them to being disillusioned and disheartened later. While there is more to communication than appears on the surface and more obstacles in the way than we like to acknowledge, it is, nevertheless, true that words need not be spoken in vain. Barriers to communication can be broken through. Meeting of meaning can occur, and through the meeting relationships can be established, even raised from the dead. These same possibilities hold also for those professionally engaged in communication. Preachers, for instance, should not have to justify themselves, as many of them do, with the pious observation that if a sermon has reached only one person its purpose has been served. Communication is not that impossible or inefficient. In spite of difficulties, it is still possible to speak and be heard, to be spoken to and to hear.

We come now to a consideration of the content of the meaning barrier. The chief ground out of which barriers grow is the need and concern which each individual feels for his own *being*—in other words, out of man's ontological need. Every person, because he is both finite and burdened with a sense of guilt, lives with anxiety in relation to known and unknown threats to his being. As one man said, "I'm not afraid of dying or of death, but what gets me is the question as to whether there is anything after death. It seems inconceivable that I should ever not be, and yet there seem to be so many things in life that are against my being. Even in me, there is something that sometimes wants to fold up and quit." We are all looking, as was this man, for guarantees and reassurances of being, and for the courage to go on being. This search for affirmation and reassurance sometimes draws us nearer to our fellows; at other times it separates and alienates us from them. Our self-concern not only sets us apart from our brothers but also makes it difficult for us to communicate with them or to hear their cry in behalf of their own ontological concerns.

Our anxieties cause us to make and to attempt to find affirmations of our own being, affirmations that may indeed threaten the being of others. Our need to be drives us to live lives of self-justification which can be a cause for uneasiness, if not enmity, in our fellows. Such ontological concern, with all the anxieties that cluster around it, makes it difficult to both speak and hear openly and honestly. This barrier to communication is built into human existence and stands between man and man in every instance. There are no exemptions. Even those persons who are marvelously drawn to each other and who find communication wonderful and exciting, experience doubts, reservations, and anxieties that keep them from speaking and cause them either not to hear or to hear incorrectly. All this becomes evident in the defensive remarks, qualifications, disguises and distortions of meaning that we use in our fear of being understood, as well as in our fear of being misunderstood.

We need to be reminded, however, that our ontological concern manifests itself not only in defenses and anxieties that separate us and create barriers to communication, but expresses itself also in longing for union with one another. From it comes a drive to speak and be understood, to give and receive an acceptance that can take away the fear of being misunderstood. Because of it we need to be known and to know, to be loved and to love.

All communication is accompanied by this ontological concern, this concern for our being, and is conditioned by it. If true communication between person and person is to occur, each must accept his own and the other's need for affirmation. Their address and response must accept, as a part of its content and responsibility, not only this ontological anxiety but all the various manifestations of it which we identify as meaning barriers.

First of all, there is the barrier of language. Language is the process of knowing and being known through the use of words, and it follows that an apt use of language is essential for effective living. The thought from one mind leaps to another mind by means of words. In back of words, however, is the whole life of relationship out of which meanings come and for which identifying words are chosen.

Speaking a word is an act that refers to and describes an event that either has occurred or is to occur. Every word, therefore, depends for its existence and meaning on life that has been lived, and every word spoken carries implicitly a responsibility for life that is to *be* lived.

But language is not exact and precise. The same word, for instance, can have different meaning for different persons even though long usage has made standard its meaning. Allowance must always be made, however, for wide ranges of nuances and variations born of individual associations and experiences. The word "father," for example, has standard meaning, but each person brings to it his own special meanings which may vary so much that its use is no guarantee of communication. A word means what the speaker intends it to mean, but the personal equivalences for the hearer may differ. This difference is found to arise primarily out of the emotional associations that have gathered around the word as a result of the hearer's particular experiences. The communicator, therefore, chooses his words with care, is careful about syntactical construction, but also is alert to possible deep emotional responses to the words he is using. The cognitive meanings of communication can be blocked by the emotional associations activated by them. Verbal communication, like an iceberg, has its vast hidden areas. Indeed, what appears on the surface is but a small part of what is involved in communication. We have all had the experience of speaking and being completely puzzled by the response we receive because it seems to be either out of proportion to what we have said or completely irrelevant. The explanation, if it were to be known, would be found in the hidden depths of the meanings activated by conscious verbal activity. These hidden depths influence not only the reception of communication but also its initiation. The speaker may have planned to say one thing but he distorts it both by the kinds of words he chooses and the tone of voice with which he uses them, and this of course may activate comparable emotional responses in the hearer.

Emotional accompaniments to language present complications for communication. Some professions, such as medicine and the ministry, have particular difficulty in this area. Such words as "hospital," "operation," "sickness," can arouse so much emotional response that people hear them as a death sentence rather than as healing, health, and life. Most ministers, if they are observant and honest, discover that biblical and theological language often is uncongenial to contemporary man who neither receives nor conveys meanings by the use of them. Common words like "love" are not effective instruments of meaning. One layman referred to the word "love" as an omnibus word, complaining that he never knew what people meant by it. He wished it could be used more definitively. Words and concepts such as "creation," "fall," "heaven," "hell," "kingdom," "resurrection," "ascension," "redemption," are meaningless to thousands of people, including life-long church members. And yet this is the language in which ministers have been trained, and they are baffled to discover the ineffectiveness of it for communication. This does not suggest that traditional words should be abandoned, but those who use them have discovered that they have a twofold responsibility: first, to explain the original meaning of the terms used; and second, to help people relate that meaning to their lives today. This should be the responsibility of the communicator in every field.

Referring to Diagram A again, what we have said about

language helps us to understand that while it is an aid to communication, it can also be a barrier. Whenever anyone seeks to speak to another he needs to use as much skill as he possesses in the use of language and yet be aware that the very words he so carefully chooses may block the effectiveness of his communication. The blocking may come from him or from the one to whom he is speaking, but more probably from both. The answer to this kind of problem will be discussed in the next chapter.

Images are another barrier to the meeting of meaning. The images which participants in communication have of one another or of the subject matter can effectively obstruct the communication. This happens when what another says has to filter through what we think he is like and, therefore, what we think he is saying. On one occasion, for example, an Episcopal minister and a Southern Baptist minister distorted almost everything said by the other because of their preconceptions about each other. When each found what the other was really like, when the image blocks of each were broken down, a relationship of trust developed between them and true communication took place. Frequently a citizen from the United States traveling abroad has encountered images of him that people in other countries have acquired through American movies. Until the traveler can break through that image with what he really is, communication between the American and the foreigners may be difficult, if not impossible, because of distortions. When what is communicated has to filter through such images, communication *is* distorted and person is separated from person. The problem is: how do we break through these images so that real communication can occur?

The respective anxieties of the partners to communication are a third barrier that keeps them from speaking and responding to one another with meaning. These can be either personal anxieties or anxieties about the subject matter.

Teachers and ministers seem to suffer widely from what I call "agenda anxiety," the anxiety to get across all the points of whatever subject they are dealing with, regardless of the state of being of those whom they are teaching. For them communication means covering the subject matter to their satisfaction. Unfortunately, one can be satisfied with his coverage of content and still fail to communicate. People have been heard to exclaim after a lecture, "Wasn't that wonderful!" But when they were asked what the lecturer said, they had to admit that they did not remember. The destructive element in agenda anxiety is that we are more concerned about data and its comprehensive coverage than we are about truth. Content is important and every communicator should deal with it responsibly, but anxiety about it should not become a barrier to the effective communication between teacher and learner. Much more important is the meeting between the meanings of a person's life and the meaning of the truth being conveyed, for the meaning of content depends upon this meeting for realization.

Sometimes we are provoked to agenda anxiety because of personal anxiety, the anxiety about ourselves and our roles as communicators, which betrays us into violating the principles of communication. Our anxiety often keeps us from being attentive to the person with whom we are speaking. This, in turn, may provoke his anxieties and make it more difficult for him to remain open to the meanings that we are trying to present.

The anxieties that we have just been discussing lead to a fourth barrier, namely, defensiveness. All of us, because we are human and vulnerable, function with certain well-established defenses in the interest of our personal and professional well-being. Self-justification is a common one. Projection, which is to blame others for something for which one is responsible, is another, as when a wife, for instance, blames her frustrations as communicator on the dumbness and unresponsiveness of her husband. Clinging to prejudice may be a defense against the disturbance of truth. Compulsive talking may be a way of avoiding what others are trying to tell us. Many people are so unsure of themselves as persons, so insecure in their function, so anxious about making themselves clear and being understood that they heap word upon word with the hope that some of what they say will convey their meaning. Their meaning, however, is buried under a mountain of words. Defensiveness of all kinds blocks communication, and communicators have to assume responsibility for its inevitable existence on both sides.

A fifth barrier to the meeting of meaning is to be found in the holding of contrary purposes. A husband may be interested only in securing agreement with his point of view, whereas his wife may be trying to think out her position and may resent, and therefore resist, his domination. Thus the good things that he has to say do not reach her, and her purposes do not become available to him for his assistance.

Thus the problems of language, images, anxieties, defenses, and purposes all exist as barriers to the meeting of meaning and as blocks to the accomplishment of the purposes of communication. And as we have seen, they are psychological and emotional symptoms of the deeper barrier which is the ontological one, our concern for our being.

Monologue: A Common Misconception
of Communication

Not only are people unaware of, and unprepared to deal with, the meaning barriers just described, but they also misconceive the nature of communication itself. Many have the concept that communication is accomplished by telling people what they ought to know. This monological illusion about communication is widely prevalent. A mother said, "I have told him a hundred times, and he still doesn't know what I'm talking about." A teacher complained, after grading examination papers, "It is obvious from these papers that my students were inattentive because I explained the material to them simply and with great care." Young ministers are disillusioned about the effectiveness of preaching and suspect that "telling" is not a sure means of communication, but because they know of no alternative they are caught in the one-way street of monologue.

In monological communication the speaker is so preoccupied with himself that he loses touch with those to whom he is speaking. To use the preacher as an illustration: he is so preoccupied with the content of his message, his purposes, and his delivery, that he is blind and deaf to the needs of his people and their search for meaning. A certain preacher commended to his congregation the practice of unqualified love and proceeded to describe what he meant by love in abstract terms, without any references to the complexities and ambiguities in which his hearers lived. After the service a man who worked for industry in the area of labor relations commented that the preacher had described a beautiful idea but added, "It just wouldn't work because life is too rough and tough." It was plain that the meanings of the preacher did not meet whatever meanings this man brought to the hearing of the sermon with the result that its message was repudiated. The preacher was concerned with an important truth; the layman was concerned with an important problem. The preacher obviously did not communicate to the parishoner, and the parishoner did not hear the preacher. In the course of a discussion following the sermon, however, the man said that in his job at the bargaining table it was necessary for him to keep the person of his opponent in focus, to respect him and his point of view, and to expect that if they worked through the various images they had of each other and through the difficulties of communication, some creative solution of their problem would be achieved. He went on to explain that one of the primary results of the bargaining process could be the improved relationship that emerged between the parties as persons. In his own words and out of the meanings of his own life this man said the same thing that the preacher urged upon his congregation, namely, that no matter what our situation is we must try to see and respond to the other side, the other person. Out of the rigors of one of the most difficult tasks in our culture, this man brought to the hearing of the gospel affirmations which, if they were made available to him, would prepare him to understand in real depth the relevance of I Corinthians 13 for modern industry. Unfortunately, he could not understand the message in the preacher's terms and, unfortunately, the preacher did not make the effort to help him understand the message in the man's terms. The result was that the meanings of the gospel and those of the man's life did not meet. Monologue is not effective communication.

The inadequacy of monological communication is born out by the studies made at the Institute for Advanced Pastoral Studies, reinforced by other research in the field of communication. Many teachers and ministers, however, resist these findings and even pride themselves on ignorance about communication or about how people learn, offering as defense their own prejudices in the field. And yet these same teachers are often impatient with the "dumbness" of their students, and ministers complain of the stupidity of their parishoners. But the communicator's effectiveness must in part be judged by the hearer's response in his own terms. Thus the grade on an examination paper is as relevant to the teacher as to the pupil.

Complaints about the theological and religious illiteracy of church people are numerous. The reason is not the lack of teaching by the Church, but the method of this teaching, which neither pays attention to the meanings that people bring nor checks their understanding of it in terms of their ability to communicate in their own words. When we do not make ourselves responsible and responsive to the patterns of experience and understanding that people bring to a particular learning situation, our communication is doomed to failure. The meaning barriers will defeat it.

Diagram A illustrates what happens in monologue. The speaker undertakes to convey, out of the subject matter for which he is responsible or the concern which he wishes to share, those meanings which he has selected as important for others to hear. As the arrows in the diagram indicate, he aims his communication in their direction. Between him and them, however, are the barriers to communication which we discussed earlier. And while it may be the wish of the hearer to receive the communication, within himself there are meanings and attitudes which require some modification before he can receive the meaning the speaker seeks to convey. Without the help of the communicator the hearer may not be able to effect for himself this modification of experience and its meaning, and may therefore be unable to break through the barriers. If the speaker is unaware of these structures in the minds or emotions of his hearers and within himself, and if he is unaware of the blocks to understanding created by these structures, no communication will take place. The academic rigidities of the preacher's concept of love and the uninterpreted meaning of the bargainer's experience at the bargaining table kept them apart until someone intervened to overcome the communication impasse, and released the meaning on one side so that it could meet the meaning on the other. But one should not have to depend upon discussion or any other technique in order to guarantee the accomplishment of communication.

This brings us to a consideration of the main question to which this book is addressed: How can the barriers to communication be overcome?

3 From Monologue to Dialogue

W E HAVE seen that in monologue a person is concerned only for himself and that, in his view, others exist to serve and confirm him. The communication of such a person is parasitical, anxious, and lacking in creative impulses and possibilities. His communication is parasitical because he is not really interested in others and values them only according to the feelings they produce in him. He is anxious because he seeks confirmation of himself, is afraid of personal encounter, and tolerates only agreement with himself and his ideas. And he is uncreative because his word is a closed, not open, one; that is, he seeks to present his own meaning as final and ultimate. The word of monologue is not only blocked by meaning barriers, but it creates them as well and, therefore, is without hope of overcoming them. In the contrast to monologue stands dialogue, on which we can focus our hope.

What Is Dialogue?

Dialogue is that address and response between persons in which there is a flow of meaning between them in spite of all the obstacles that normally would block the relationship. It is that interaction between persons in which one of them seeks to give himself as he is to the other, and seeks also to know the other as the other is. This means that he will not attempt to impose his own truth and view on the other. Such is the relationship which characterizes dialogue and is the precondition to dialogical communication. Even in the course of monologue, this relationship may emerge and change the monologue into dialogue. At some moment, in the monologue, one participant may give up his pretenses and lay aside the masks by which he seeks the approval and good will of the other, dare to be what he is in relation to the other, invite the other to be a partner in dialogue and be fully present to him as he really is. At that moment each of the participants must accept the resulting address and response as the discipline and task of communication. Any relationship less than this would not be dialogue and, therefore, not communication. Rather, it would be the exploitation of the other or the ignoring of him or flight from him.

When we talk to others with the sole purpose of getting them to do what we want, we are exploiting them. We have to make allowance, of course, for the "economic" relation between persons. In the conduct of the business of living it is necessary for us to use and be used by one another. And the well-being of children, for example, is dependent many times on their being made to do what their parents want. Obedience is one of the disciplines of living which all of us, in one way or another and at different times in our lives, must observe. The question is whether people are merely being directed and used, or whether they are first respected and valued for what they are in themselves. If they are only being used, then as persons, they are being ignored, and we are trying to appropriate them as a part of ourselves. When we refuse to hear them and thus ignore them, or when we do not hear what they say or change the subject and flee from them, we reject them. But when we really try to see them, to know them for what they are, and to speak to them honestly, we are honoring them and inviting them to respond in such a way that we can meet as persons in our communication. Every genuine conversation, therefore, can be an ontological event, and every exchange between husband and wife, parent and child, teacher and pupil, person and person, has more meaning than the thing talked about. What happens between men is of primary importance and provides an enabling or disabling context for the purpose of whatever exchange takes place between them.

"Experiencing the other side" is Buber's phrase for identifying the nature of dialogue, and by it he means to feel an event from the side of the person one meets as well as from one's own side. And so the true teacher accepts, as a part of the discipline of his profession, the responsibility to be aware of the meaning of a course from the student's point of view and to be alert to the meaning of his side of the learning situation. Education, relationships, love, and communication that are not dialogical, are evil because they exploit and seek to appropriate. Much education and communication, to say nothing of love and relationship, are evil and destructive. The same can be said for much religion when it emphasizes an attitude that turns one in on oneself. Preoccupation with one's moral state, with one's emotional life or spiritual being, is self-destroying. Jesus taught men to look not in on themselves but to the other, whether man or God; to love, to give, to affirm, to forgive, and, in so doing, to love oneself.

Only as we know another and are known by him, can we know ourselves. This is the source of the child's knowledge of himself when at last he is able to say "I," with consciousness of himself as a distinct, autonomous but related person of worth. Likewise, the mature person is enabled to say "I" out of his knowing and responding to others. We might wonder why it is important for a person to be able to say "I." Does it not have a self-centered, if not selfish, sound? Our answer is that if we are concerned about self apart from our responsible relation to others, our concern can be selfish; but when selfhood and the saying of "I" is prized for the sake of the possibility of dialogue with others, then his affirming the personal pronoun becomes the act of a man's spirit. A great man is one who is able to meet the truths and challenges of life as they are presented to him through the living and teaching of others, maintaining, however, his own unity of being, which is the source of his responsible action in behalf of others. Such a man is able to meet, confirm, and respond to those who oppose him without losing his own sense of being. And yet, he would be the first to acknowledge his dependence on the "enemy," as it were. His independence would not be defiant or aggressive because it would be the independence of dialogue; and his dependence would not be weakness or sickness but the dependence which characterizes dialogue. Being a real person, he would be capable of more completely relating his life to the life of others, and through them to the whole world of meaning and truth. His life and ours—since we also are all called to greatness of spirit—may be said to be formed and illumined by the principle of dialogue.

When this principle directs our lives, our communication becomes creative. The spoken word becomes the servant of the spirit. For some, it may be necessary to distinguish between the *principle* of dialogue and dialogue as *method.* The principle of dialogue we have already identified as openness to the other side, with a willingness not only to speak but to respond to what we hear. Without this distinction between principle and method there is the danger of misunderstanding and distortion. Some might even think that what is being urged here is the employment of a method of communication, when the truth of the matter is that we are advocates of no particular method of communication but only of the principle of dialogue as we have defined it.

Any method of communication may be the servant of the dialogical principle. A monological method can be an effective instrument of the dialogical principle, such as a creative lecture in which the lecturer is alert to and activates the meanings of his hearers in relation to what he is saying. Or a dialogical method can be used to serve a monological principle. That is the case when an "imperialist" uses the group-process method as a new way of clobbering people with his views and purposes. (He has acquired an unexpected versatility!) In other words, the communicator who is faithful to the dialogical principle may use either dialogical or monological methods of communication with creative results; he is free to use the group method or the lecture method, whichever one is appropriate for his purpose. When he uses the lecture method, however, he uses it in a dialogical context, and those whom he is teaching are being provided with an opportunity either before, during, or after the lecture to respond to him in their own terms. All of us have experienced the difference between the dialogical and the monological lecture. Certainly we have listened to lecturers and preachers who seem to draw us into an implicit dialogue with them in such a way that the meanings they bring to us activate the meanings we bring to our hearing of them. The emphasis here, then, is not on method but on the principle of dialogue.

To be deplored are the silly controversies that people engage in about methods of communication, controversies that result in people lining themselves up with this school or with that, with this method or that. They take sides as a "group process" party or as disciples of the lecture method or as devotees of the audio-visual approach to education, or of the case-study approach, with the expectation that their method will answer the problems of communication and of education. It is as ridiculous to separate ourselves into these methodological schools as it would be for carpenters to divide themselves into tool schools, so that one carpenter might say, "I am a hammer man"; another, "I am a plane man"; and still another, "I am a saw man." The educational structures that we build by this preposterous "tool" loyalty are as bizarre and useless as would be a house built by someone who used only a hammer. It is foolish to choose tools because of our preference for one or another of them, instead of choosing them in the context of the principle that informs their purposes as well as their methods. Furthermore, our choice of tools should be made in relation to the task to be performed, a choice made freer when the communicator is serving the dialogical principle. By this we mean that if a question needs to be asked, a method should be used that will help people to formulate their question. This would seem to indicate something approximating the group process. If, however, the question has been asked and an answer is needed, some method should be used that provides the answer in response to the implicit or explicit question, and this might be a lecture.

The communicator, be he teacher, labor leader, husband, or parent, should first be clear about the principle on which communication depends and then use as many tools as are needed for the accomplishment of his task. We need to be versatile in the use of methods. A common basic criticism made of many of us is that we have become stereotyped with respect to our understanding of the methods of communication.

The employment of the dialogical principle calls for correlative thinking; a thinking that looks for reciprocal relations between things, between persons, between meanings and truths, between theory and practice, between little meanings and ultimate meanings. When we are studying a theory, we should at the same time be thinking in terms of life situations and questions to which it applies and which test it.

The greatest of teachers, Jesus of Nazareth, used both the dialogical principle and correlative thinking, as his parables and his conversations with people show. Take, for example, the conversation of Jesus with the woman at the well, and notice how he moved in his conversation with her from a consideration of the water that quenches physical thirst to the Living Water, from a theoretical discussion about religion to a consideration of the kind of life that the woman was living.

The dialogical principle with its employment of correlative thinking lies at the basis of his parables. And we need to employ it in our own time. Actually, people need help in recasting the parables in contemporary terms. A literal-minded business man, for instance, claimed he could not understand the parable of the pearl of great price in which the merchant of pearls sold all his pearls in order to gain the most beautiful one he had ever seen. When he was asked whether he had ever done a comparable thing in his business, he remembered that he had often sold certain stocks in order to buy others which, in his judgment, would prove to be of much greater value.

We might also create our own parables. A teacher* addressed a mixed group of children and adults on the subject of baptism by beginning with the observation that baptism is like a home in which some puppies were born. He went on to explain that these puppies were fortunate because they had a devoted mother who kept them warm and fed them and was in every way a good mother. They had been born into a dog world that was as loving and competent as any puppy could expect. But the puppies' world was dependent on another world. Who, for instance, was going to take care of the mother? Who was going to feed her and give

* The Rt. Rev. Robert DeWitt, in an address at Christ Church Cranbrook, Bloomfield Hills, Michigan.

her a home? Who was going to watch over her care of her babies in order to make sure that her mother-dog care was good for the puppies and that they would be saved from the effects of her ignorance? The human world into which these puppies were born saw to it that their mother was fed and given a home. And so it is with us. We are born into our own families that in many ways are competent to take care of us, but we are also born into God's family who watches over our human family, saves us from the sins and failures of our human parents, and completes the love that we have from them. By means of this parable the meaning of baptism, difficult for a child to understand, was conveyed to them in terms of their understanding of the puppies' situation. Furthermore, they were being trained to think correlatively and were learning to move to and fro between the meaning of everyday events and the great truths that illumine human life.

The Power of Dialogue to Overcome Barriers

Monologue, as we have seen, is not only unable to breach the barriers to a meeting of meaning but even creates them because it does not take the other person seriously. In monologue, communication becomes only a juggling of opinions. Dialogue, on the other hand, because it takes the other person seriously, causes language to become the means to a genuine meeting between persons in which the conversation is a vehicle of re-creation. We turn now to an examination of how dialogue acts in relation to barriers.

Diagram B, based on Diagram A used in Chapter 2, represents the action of dialogue as the participants in a "conversation" address each other. As in Diagram A, the

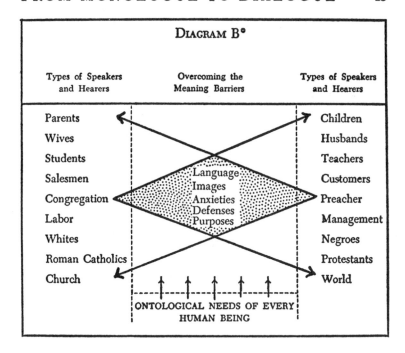

DIAGRAM B*

| Types of Speakers and Hearers | Overcoming the Meaning Barriers | Types of Speakers and Hearers |

Parents — Children
Wives — Husbands
Students — Teachers
Salesmen — Customers
Congregation — Preacher
Labor — Management
Whites — Negroes
Roman Catholics — Protestants
Church — World

Language
Images
Anxieties
Defenses
Purposes

ONTOLOGICAL NEEDS OF EVERY HUMAN BEING

participants listed on either side of Diagram B may be either speakers or hearers; each participant brings certain meanings (values, attitudes, understandings) to the encounter; each, out of his ontological need, seeks the other; but each, because of his need, will act and speak in ways that can alienate and set up barriers to possible meetings of persons and meanings; and each finds his communication blocked by the existence of language difficulties, images, anxieties, defenses, and contrary purposes. The barrier, however, is a perforated, not solid, one; so we do manage to get through

* I am indebted to the Rev. H. William Foreman, Jr., Rector, Trinity Church, Fayetteville, New York, for this diagram which modifies in part my own.

to each other on occasion, but we may not understand why we have succeeded in communicating any more than, at other times, we understand why we have failed. Our thesis here is that we can know why we fail and learn how we can communicate more dependably.

Participants on either side in Diagram B may initiate or resume the dialogue; and this holds true as a possibility for groups as well as individuals, and it is a necessity if the relations between individuals and groups are to be real. Once dialogue is initiated, the speaker must accept both his responsibility and a readiness to be flexible. He has the responsibility to represent what he knows and believes, namely, to witness to the truth he has received. The readiness to be flexible is required of him because he faces the possibility that the questions or responses of the person to whom he speaks may force him on reflection to change his own views. Each side of the dialogue speaks to the other; and, in the diagram, the addresses and responses of each side are represented by the two sets of arrows shaped like cones or megaphones. In dialogue each side speaks with "openness" to the other side. Where the two cones intersect, real hearing or meeting of meaning takes place. But because the word spoken in dialogue is an open word, there is the possibility that a hearing and meeting of meaning may continue indefinitely, so that even years later when the participants are no longer addressing one another, the area of intersection will grow. Former students of the author have written to him many years after the teacher-student relationship had terminated to acknowledge the continued growth and understanding which they were experiencing and which, in their minds, was associated with our dialogue of some years before.

A simple illustration may help us to understand the process. A certain man hired an architect to design a house for him. When the plans were presented, the client looked them over and made some suggestions which would require changes. The architect protested on the grounds that he was the architect and, therefore, knew more about planning a house than did the client. The architect was discharged. Thus far, we have an illustration of monologue in which the architect was not interested in the "other side," namely, the man who had asked for the house plan. The architect's ontological concerns made him anxious, called out his defenses, and caused him to have difficulty with his image of himself as an authority, and made his purpose antagonistic to his client's. There were also misunderstandings due to language difficulties. Obviously, the sides did not intersect and there was no hearing or meeting of meaning.

The client then invited a second architect to submit a design. When the new plan was presented, the client again made suggestions requiring changes. The new architect listened to him, discussed with him the various possibilities, and after a period of study and further discussion presented a completely new set of plans. These were accepted, and when the construction of the house was completed, the architect said to his client, "This is one of the best houses I have ever designed, but just as important is the relationship that has grown up between us." Here we have dialogue that produced mutual hearing and achievement.

Because the client and the second architect were human, both had ontological concerns which were expressed in the language and images they used, and in the anxieties, defenses, and struggling purposes they entertained. The difference between the client's two experiences, however, lay in the second architect's acceptance of these concerns as a part of the exchange. The client committed his hopes for his house to this architect and was open to his ideas without surrendering his own. This architect, in turn, committed his hopes as an architect to his client, and although he had confidence in his training and ability, he could accept the possibility that his client's suggestions might help him design and build a better house. Each, then, lived in relation to the other side and, in doing so, not only rendered service to but cared for each other, so that in the end they felt that they had not only built a good house but had met as persons. In this way the diagram represents an important truth, namely, that communication is accomplished not when the barriers are wiped away, but when they are accepted as a part of the communication. We often hear people make the statement: "There's no point in my talking to you; you don't want to understand." We now see that it is precisely because there is a lack of understanding that it is imperative that the effort to communicate be maintained. The resistance to understanding has to be accepted as a part of the dialogue. It becomes the curriculum of the dialogue—that is, a part of its very subject matter. When the two sides are willing to accept this curriculum, there is the real possibility that the dialogue will accomplish its miracles.

The diagram also helps to make clear that communication does not take place in a vacuum but rather that the participants must accept the barriers and assail them from both sides. One reason for so little progress in the development of the relationship between races, for example, is that there is a reluctance on both sides to accept the barriers as a part of the problem and to deal with them together. The whole question of equality raises the ontological question again. *Being* is threatened for one side if there is equality, and for the other side if there is not equality. From this threat to being emerge barriers of language, such as the words "nigger," "segregation," "education," "polls," which have the power to accent and solidify separation; and such images as "marry your sister"; or such anxieties as those connected with property values in relation to open occupancy; and such defenses and avoidance of responsibility as the blaming of others for the disruptive situation. These barriers are accepted as a justification of the separation, and many on both sides rejoice in the rigidities of language and images that keep the races apart so that anxieties are fed, defenses strengthened, and purposes confused. Until both sides can be open to one another and help one another over their ontological concerns, and the meaning barriers that emerge out of them, strained relations will continue.

The same condition marked the relations between the Protestant and Roman Catholic churches. Until a few years ago the rigid language, concepts, and images of both produced only monological approaches. Each considered the other as an object to be misrepresented and proselytized. Now, however, the situation is beginning to change and mutual respect is appearing. To some extent, each is beginning to regard the other as a partner, someone to be taken seriously, whose point of view must be understood and whose meanings must be examined; both are aware of the possibility that the meanings of one may cause those of the other to be revised. Language and concepts are being brought under the greater judgment of truths. Images are being broken through and displaced by the efforts to meet and see the other as it really is. This diminishes the anxieties, makes defenses less necessary, and leaves both sides open for a reconsideration of their respective purposes. We are witnessing a resumption of dialogue between Protestants and Roman Catholics which may very well produce miracles that a hundred years ago seemed impossible.

In conclusion, we have distinguished between the dialogical principle and the dialogical method. Dialogue is a reciprocal relationship in which each party "experiences the other side" so that their communication becomes a true address and response in which each informs and learns. This is the principle that underlies true communication and is not dependent upon any one method. The dialogical method is but one of many, and while it usually serves the dialogical principle, it is not to be confused with it.

4 The Purpose of Dialogue

W<small>E OFTEN</small> do things without regard for purpose, assuming that we know why we are doing them. This is true of our communications. We converse with one another, day after day, about all sorts of things, without ever wondering what purpose our exchange serves or should serve. Sometimes our purpose may be unworthy of so rare a privilege as communication. Certainly, anyone who is at all observant can easily gain the impression that for many people talk is indeed cheap.

Let us consider, first, some inadequate purposes of dialogue, and, second, the true purposes which it is intended to serve.

Two Inadequate Purposes

The pursuit of inadequate purposes in communication results in its abuse. Every good use of things can be turned into an abuse; and so, too, the useful possibilities of communication can also go unrealized or become corrupted.

1. The purpose of communication is not to give our answers to people's questions. When we have been asked, "What would you do if you were in my place?" we often comment later, "I didn't know what to tell him." Implicit in that response is the assumption that we should have known and told the inquirer what he should do. We are all tempted to think of ourselves as potential dispensers of answers to people's questions. Certainly, this is true of those who are regarded as authorities in some field of study or action. When a question is put to an authority, he often answers what is being asked instead of using his knowledge, understanding, and skill to help his inquirers move in the direction of finding answers to their own questions. The image of himself as an authority seems to require that he exercise his authority in this primitive, naïve way rather than in more creative and educative ways. He has not discovered the greater excitement and satisfaction of having learners experience for themselves, with guidance, of course, the joy of acquiring insight and knowledge. Because teachers so often rush to give their own answers and opinions to questions, instead of using their resources to help others learn, much that passes for education weakens the student rather than strengthens him, and makes him more dependent rather than more resourceful. This has been the effect of much theological education on candidates for the ministry during

their training period. Many ministers complain today that their teachers thought and spoke for them, and now that they have the responsibility of leadership, they are unable to exercise true authority because they were trained to be dependent upon the authority of others; and as a result, they feel uncomfortable and guilty now about the authority that goes with their office. When they are forced to assume authority, they have no alternative but to practice the same version of it as demonstrated by their teachers. Too much of our educational endeavor seems to be aimed at turning out a generation of scribes and conformists rather than people who, having acquired the power to study, think, and decide for themselves, can speak as having authority.

There is no reason at all why we should provide people with answers to their questions, although the temptation to do so is very great. A husband and wife with a problem which they found most perplexing consulted a minister with the request that he tell them what they should do. The wife, in this case, had contracted measles during her pregnancy, and the best medical prediction was that the baby would be born defective. The couple had three other children. Their physician recommended that she have a medical abortion. The wife wanted it, the husband did not. They had not been able to make up their minds. The time in which such an operation would be possible had almost passed, and only one week remained in which to make a decision. Unable to make up their minds, they came to their pastor, asking him what they ought to do. At first, the minister was panicked by the question; then he realized that it was not his responsibility to give them an answer. The decision was their responsibility, and it was his to listen, to introduce helpful information, to raise questions that would stimulate their thinking, and generally to help them use every available resource that would assist them in arriving at their own answer. The giving of answers to other people's questions is a thankless task. If the answer given turns out to be wrong, they will resent both the answer and the one who gives it; and if it turns out to be right, they may also be resentful because they themselves did not think of it. In any event, this couple would have been greatly weakened in their capacity to live their own lives if their minister had given them an answer to their question and they had acted on it. Instead, he fulfilled his responsibility to them by helping them make their own decision.

The conclusion to be drawn here is not that one should not supply essential information. The couple, for example, asked whether the Church was against medical abortion, and the minister informed them that Protestant churches generally do not take a stand against it and hold the opinion that since it is a medical problem, it should be decided by responsible medical authorities.

When a question is asked that calls for essential information, it is only sensible that an answer be given. An interesting shift has occurred recently in our understanding of these matters. Some teachers, for example, as a result of the emphasis on the group process of teaching, have moved from the old authoritarian role to the new permissive non-directive role with the result that many of them now involve their students *ad nauseum* in the formulation of questions because they are afraid to provide the information which the questions demand. Ministers also express anxiety at finally answering a question: "I feel guilty that I told them something they needed to know." Parents, likewise, have been intimidated by this emphasis on making the child responsible and often fail to step in decisively when action on their part is called for. Apparently, we have been removed from one horn of the dilemma and impaled on the other. Escape from this dilemma is to be found in the employment of the dialogical principle which brings people with their knowledge, skills, and purpose into complementary relation with one another. This means that the parent assumes his responsibility in relation to the child but does not usurp the child's responsibility. The teacher carries out his role but refuses to act in place of the student. The minister, likewise, takes his part but does not presume to tell the parishoner what he should think or do.

2. Another misconception about the purpose of communication is that of securing consensus with the point of view of the communicator. Agreement is not the aim of communication. Agreement there may be, but it should come as a result of independent, self-deciding participation in a process that leads up to it. On the other hand, communication that seeks to gain agreement may do violence to the persons who are led to agree. The failure to leave men free to their own response by forcing them to agree to a course of action can be tragic. I know a man who prides himself on the number of young men he has persuaded to enter the ministry. They gave assent to his decision for them without having opportunity to really consider alternatives. Their preparation for the ministry required that they reconsider their decision in order that it might become their own, and when many of them discovered that they had been pressured into a commitment that they were not ready to assume, they wisely left seminary

for another vocation. The purpose of communication is not to seduce or exploit persons but to bring them into responsible relation to the world of persons and things. Agreement between persons can be deadly—as many a marriage testifies. The purpose of communication in a marriage is not to get the partners to agree but to bring them into relation in which the uniqueness of each stands in a complementary relation to the other. And this is possible even when there is disagreement.

If it is not the purpose of communication to answer people's questions and to achieve consensus with a point of view, what are the purposes of communication?

The Purposes of Communication

1. Communication is a means by which information and meaning is conveyed and received between individuals and groups. As we have seen, either the language of words or the language of relationship serves that purpose. Dialogue calls for collaborative, complementary use of the two languages in order that words about a truth may be embodied in a relationship which is concerned with that truth. If two people or two parties are trying to work out a difference in order that some kind of adjusted relationship may be achieved, as in the case of a labor dispute, there must be embodied in each a willingness to understand the problem from the other side as well as from his own. And this willingness will be expressed in the spirit and manner of each party as they come together for that purpose. This requires no diminution of devotion to one's own cause, but it does require seeing one's own cause in relation to other points of view which are its context.

One of the first and more simple purposes of communication is to make available to people the knowledge and skill that has accumulated from the study and experience of generations of men. Communication is not primarily or exclusively concerned with contemporary experiences between persons; it is equally concerned with the formulation, assimilation, and dissemination of the accumulated knowledge about the world of persons and things and with the ultimate meaning of them. We need to remember, however, that content about the world and its meaning is the product of the living and thinking of men. The propositional formulations of life and thought must be studied and held in responsible relation to the requirements of contemporary life. Content separated from experience becomes lifeless form, and experience separated from the disciplines of content becomes formless life.

2. A second purpose of communication is to help persons make a responsible decision, whether that decision be Yes or No in relation to the truth that is being presented. This purpose stands in sharp contrast to the one more commonly held, namely, to persuade persons toward a point of view. Incidentally, this purpose is consistent with the necessity that was mentioned earlier that dialogue keep each party free to make his own response. Communication is successful when either a responsible negative or affirmative response has been made. A decision to say No is as much a part of dialogue as a decision to say Yes. Most of us, however, feel that our communication has failed unless it elicits an affirmative decision, one that is in agreement with our point of view.

Because the word of dialogue is an open word which accepts as relevant all that is seriously said, it maintains a different attitude toward negative and critical responses than does monologue which, by its very nature, finds denial intolerable. Dialogue has more respect for a responsible No and all that it signifies than for an irresponsible Yes. Because monologue seeks always to speak the concluding word, a negative response is seen to have no future and must therefore stand as a sign of failure in communication. The word of dialogue, on the other hand, since it is a beginning word, is able to accept the negative response as part of the dialogue, and instead of regarding it as a sign of failure sees it as a part of the process in which a person moves from one point of view or conviction to another. It is necessary for us sometimes to say No before we can say Yes. We see this truth in the lives of our children. When asked to do something they often refuse vehemently and then later give assent. Saying No may be a declaration of independence by means of which the youngster tries to make sure that he is his own person as over against the adult whose persuasiveness and authority threatens to overwhelm him. Then having made sure that he is his own person, the child becomes free to say Yes, and both his Yes and No are more responsible, the No being a necessary prelude to a significant Yes.

When a No has been said, in a conversation between friends (or in an exchange between parent and child, or husband and wife, or teacher and pupil, or minister and parishoner, or employer and employee), the partner in the communication should try to make sure that the person making the negative response means what he says. The person may need assistance in making sure that his No is responsible and not emotional. With children it is often necessary to ask them directly whether they really mean to take the position they have, and then to try to help them understand the consequences. If they persist, then within protective limits they should experience the results of their decision.

The same is true, of course, for the adult. A certain man, for example, who, under the pressure of several complicated problems—too much work, fatigue, a sense of inadequacy—told a friend that he was going to abandon his business in the midst of an important project, leave his wife and family, and go off somewhere to find peace. His dialogue with life had produced in him a need to shout No to everything. The friend was able to accept his need to say No because of his understanding of the man's desperate situation, but he was not sure that the man really meant what he said or was saying what he really meant. So he said to his friend, "Suppose you do make this decision and walk off and leave everything, how will you feel five years from now about having done so? Will you feel then that your decision was right for you, or will you discover that you did not really mean to say No to everything?" The question caused the man to reconsider his response to his life and to find ways and means of continuing with his responsibilities. He had been in danger of saying an irresponsible No and the dialogue of his friend helped him to see that danger and to change his No to a Yes.

He might have carried out his original negative response. The consequences of having done so would then have become a part of his dialogue; and as he confronted the implications of these in his living, they too would become a part of his dialogue with life. When King Edward said No to the British throne and Yes to the woman he loved, his proposed decision was tested by several of his advisors, who in effect were asking: Do you really mean to say No to your kingly responsibilities in order that you may say Yes to this woman? The question might have caused him to change his response, but it did not. He persisted, the course of history was changed, and his No to the throne and Yes to his love changed the content of the dialogue of his life.

These insights have meaning for everyday life. In our dialogue we help one another to say what we mean, and to make sure that we mean what we say. Once this is done, then there must be acceptance of the response and commitment to the consequences as a necessary part of our living life together.

Another aspect of this purpose of communication is to help people realize that when they say No to one thing they are saying Yes to others, and that when they say Yes to something they must inevitably also be saying No to contrary things. The prevalence of ambiguity in so many people's lives is due, in large measure, to lack of sharpness in their decisions. They know neither what they are saying Yes to nor, therefore, what they should be saying No to.

The decision to save money, for example, means that one has to say No to spending it for many of the things one would like to buy. Unfortunately, we like to have our cake and eat it too. We are not prepared for the denials that have to accompany our affirmations. We may think that we have made a decision for democracy, to use another illustration, but we discover that while we pride ourselves on living in a country founded on democratic principles, we ourselves are living monologically and imperialistically. This means that we have given a verbal and superficial Yes to the democratic faith we thought we held and an undecided, practicing Yes to the contrary principle that allows the exploitation and manipulation of persons.

Another example can be found in church membership and preparation for it. All churches of whatever denomination have some form for receiving their members which, in a variety of ways, requires the new member to promise to follow Jesus Christ as his Lord and Savior. But preparation for this membership is such that people are allowed to say Yes to him and his service without really knowing what that assent means, and without knowing to what, by implication, they are saying No, and what these denials will mean in their living. Both a study of church membership courses and a questioning of church members reveal an ambiguity that explains the lack of clarity and courage in the Church's witness in the world. The courses often indicate that the Christian faith is presented in isolation from any other point of view, with the result that people decide to be Christians without really having made any choice because no alternatives were considered. When questioned about this matter ministers often reply that they are afraid to present people with a choice for fear they will choose against Christianity and thus be lost to church membership. There is reason to believe, however, that many people whose names are on the church rolls are not really members because they do not know what they believe and should stand for, and certainly their practice would suggest that they are really members of an altogether different fellowship. They have not been prepared to the point where their Yes can be yes, and their No, no.

Conviction can only be born out of a dialogue between alternatives. How tragic it is to think that we are "preparing" a group of young people for church membership when, at the same time, we are not guiding them in a study of some of the live alternatives to Christianity, such as secularism and Communism. Did we do so, they would be helped to consider the appeals of secularism, humanism, Communism, and Christianity, and they would also be guided in the consideration of the difficulties and pains of being Christian as well as of the limitations and error of other positions. In one instance an apathetic group of young churchpeople became convinced and excited Christians when the Christian position was brought for them into dialogue with some of its alternatives. For a period of a year or two several of them gave their allegiance to the Communist point of view. The leader of the group and the group itself, however, kept the dialogue going, and in time the young people in question moved from a Communist position to the one that had its sources in Christianity.

The presence of moralism among Christian people is evident when they say Yes to being Christian but do not really know to what they are giving assent. By *moralism* we mean the conviction that one is a Christian by reason of one's own moral efforts, in contrast to the truth that one becomes a Christian by accepting what was done for him by Christ. A Christian's ethic is, then, a "therefore" or "thank you" one, not a self-righteous, self-justifying one. These people who, in the name of Christianity, give assent to self-righteousness and salvation by works, say No to Christ and all he stood for by their lack of forgiveness to people who sin and run into all kinds of trouble. Because our communication is used to promote premature and superficial assent, and the loyalties and issues of the Christian profession are not made clear, the Christian Church is kept from being the fellowship of forgiveness that it is meant to be; and it cannot, therefore, fulfill the only mission that can possibly justify its existence and claim. Our Lord was concerned that our Yes should be yes and our No, no. We need to remember his parable about the men who were asked to work in a vineyard. One said that he would, but he did not; another said that he would not, but he did. The Yes of the first man was irresponsible; the No of the second man led to a Yes.

The purpose of dialogue, therefore, is to translate the word into action. Assent must be incarnate in the life of the person.

3. Another purpose of communication, and therefore of dialogue, is to bring back the forms of life into relation to the vitality which originally produced them. Life always expresses itself in some form, and every form gives evidence of the vitality that produced it. The vitality of love between a man and woman moves them toward the form known as marriage. And every marriage witnesses to the vitality that produced it even though it may no longer serve it. The normal state of relationship between life and the form that expresses it is one of tension. Many people think that tension means conflict. Tension may produce conflict, but is not itself conflict. For example, when violin strings have the right tension, they can be used to produce music. Similarly, when a creative tension exists between the vitality of a relationship and the form of its life, the relationship is a growing one in which the partners are being renewed and transformed.

Because tension is painful, we want to get rid of it, and we may do so by choosing the forms of life instead of life itself. This process lies back of our nostalgic longing for the "good old days." A wife of a successful and busy man often looks back longingly to the early days of their life when they were able to spend more time together in pursuing their mutual interests and planning their future. There is a desire to go back to that form of their life instead of accepting the opportunities, resources, and problems of the present with a readiness to achieve new forms for their living. Resentment of change very often keeps people from accepting present possibilities. But the possibilities of the present cannot be accepted unless there is a willingness to accept the tensions between vitality and form and to take the risk of creativity, the risk in trying to find new forms equal to the vitality of the present.

The purpose of dialogue, therefore, is to restore the tension between vitality and form, to bring parties of a relationship into communicative relation with one another, to shake them free of their conformity and make them available for transformation. Only through dialogue can the miracle of renewal be accomplished in a relationship.

Forms and patterns in church life also tend to hold captive the vitality of the Church. The forms of worship, for example, may become substitutes for life and for the spirit of worship. A lack of tension between the spirit and the forms of worship can produce a dead and sterile church which is one that, like the Pharisee, stands and prays with itself. Such a church has lost its sense of relation with all else, including God whom it professes to serve and the world to which it is sent. The miracle of renewal can occur only when the Church turns to its task, namely, living for its Lord dialogically with the world. It must have the courage and determination to sustain the tension between the source of its life and its task. The purpose of dialogue is to bring the meanings that come out of men's living in the world to a meeting of the meanings that come out of the encounter between God and man in Christ. Men must bring their hopes and purposes, their achievements and failures, their triumphs and their sins, what they are and what they are not, and offer them as a part of their worship to the One who gave all that he had in his love for man. The dialogue of worship thus conceived becomes the dialogue of living; and the Church is just as much the Church when, in its members, it stands at the work bench or sits in the office or plows in the field as when it kneels before the altar.

4. A final purpose of dialogue is to bring persons into being. Man becomes man in personal encounter, but personal encounter requires address and response between person and person. Man has dominion over the created world, and there is no limit there that can bind him. But he cannot have dominion in the world of the personal. He must meet the other person as an equal. The person who stands over against him limits him, and the other person cannot be removed, fathomed, or exploited. If we try to do so, we will destroy ourselves. The person of the other demands, by his very existence, that he be acknowledged as a *thou* in his own right, as a *thou* to my *I* and as an *I* to himself. If we try to do anything other than to meet this person, his resistance will force us either to take him seriously as a person or to find some escape from the encounter with him. We may do this in a number of ways. For instance, we may construct an image of him that is compatible with our need and then relate to him as if he were that construct rather

than himself. Or we may escape by trying to surrender our own ego integrity to his and pretend a compatibility that cannot possibly exist. Dialogue offers the only possibility for a relation between the *thou* of the other person and the *I* of myself. I can only speak to him and leave him free to respond, and out of that exchange we may both be called forth as persons in a relationship of mutual trust. The only hope for the restoration of persons who have attempted escape by either image-building or ego-sacrificing is their recovery of the power of dialogue which makes these kinds of escapes unnecessary.

This, then, is the purpose of dialogue: the calling forth of persons in order that they may be reunited with one another, know the truth, and love God, man, and themselves. We move toward the realization of this purpose when we speak responsibly out of what we know, when we help others to say Yes and No as responsibly as possible, and when we keep the forms of our life open to life itself.

5 The Participants in Dialogue

DIALOGUE, as we have seen thus far, is both
the relationship between persons and the principle that determines the nature of their communication. The partner-
ship of persons in dialogue is so indispensably important
that we turn now to a study of the participants in it.

The Nature of the Relationship

The vocation of every man is to enter into relation with
other persons. This act of entering into relation with others
is not as easy as people generally suppose. The invitation to
be a person, which is necessary for the individual's becoming
a person, must come from another, and one must wait for
that invitation. We need to remember what Buber has
pointed out, that the invitation comes from a person who

must inevitably stand at some distance from us, because *relation* presupposes both distance (which is another way of saying "distinctness") and presentness. Young couples frequently make the mistake of assuming that love requires only intimacy, so that each strives to lose himself in the other. But such exclusive appropriation of or immersion in another destroys the possibility of relationship, the polarity necessary for dialogue, the polarity we mean by *distance*. This polarity is necessary for any genuine relationship, and certainly for a teaching or pastoral one. Both presentness and distance are especially required where education or care occurs. Each party must be a distinct and independent person if there is to be a relationship and if there is to be dialogue. Abnormal dependence of one upon the other or any blurring of the distinctness impairs the relationship and, therefore, the dialogue.

The Obliteration of Persons

The breakdown of community and, therefore, of dialogue, occurs when there is an obliteration of persons. This obliteration takes place when one person or the other exploits the relationship for any purpose other than its true one. Instances of this are commonplace. A man may cultivate a "friendship" with another for the sake of the prestige it gives him; or a parent may dominate and enjoy his child, impose upon him his own limitations of thought and feeling, or act in ways that satisfy his own vanity. When we do these things we degrade ourselves, the other, and the truth for which each has responsibility.

The obliteration of persons occurs, therefore, when there is the exploitive appropriation of one person by another and the reduction of persons to the status of things. We turn persons into things when we value and deal with them only in terms of their function or usefulness to us. When we "imagize" ourselves and others, and hide behind the façade of what we want to appear to be, then we become personages and cease to be persons; we also become incapable of dialogue. What passes now for communication is only monologue because a total honest response is not wanted or is precluded. From this it may also be seen that monologue fosters alienation and apartness, and only dialogue has the power to unite persons and bring them together.

Because it is our purpose here, however, to explore the possibilities of dialogue rather than try to rearrange the dry bones of our sins and failures into some kind of corpse for diagnosis, we turn our attention to a consideration of the person in dialogue.

The Dialogical Person

By dialogical person we mean one who, by word or relationship, is in communication with his environment and open to the communication that environment offers, environment in this sense including both persons and things. The dialogical person is a rare individual, although he need not be. He may appear in the guise of any type. He can be a poet, philosopher, scientist, artist, administrator, industrialist, or minister. Even in the midst of a competitive transaction there may pass between two persons a glance in which the eyes are instruments of deep personal meeting, and the new creation gleams in the midst of the travail of the old. What, then, are some of the characteristics of the person in dialogue, the qualities by which we may recognize him?

1. *The dialogical person is a total, authentic person.* He is one who responds to others with his whole being and not with just a part of himself, and he is able to listen with his heart as well as with his mind. He is *really* present; he does not run off on "errands" while he seems to be listening to the person before him. He is an authentic person, too, in the sense that he is able to learn as well as to teach, to accept love as well as to love, to be ministered unto as well as to minister. In other words, he is not defensive in his relations and does not have to waste his energies in protecting and defending himself. Instead, he is delighted to be in relation to his fellows and recognizes his dependence upon them. At the same time he is also independent, able to stand on his own two feet, and to distinguish between that which is himself and that which is not. The authentic person, then, is one who sees the one before him as a person to whom he can give himself rather than as an individual to be manipulated or to be gotten to accept some image of himself which the speaker may be trying to "get across."

I once had a teacher who used his students as an audience to reflect his image of himself as a clever teacher. He *was* clever, but we did not learn anything under him. The authentic teacher, however, is one who is free to choose, initiate, and think because he is free to act constructively out of an inner core of character in relation to the variety, complexity, and ambiguity of his world. The teacher's world is made up, on the one hand, of his students, and on the other, of phenomena and their meaning. He has to be steady in relation to the incompleteness and uncertainty of his students' knowledge and understanding and of the difficulties that they must endure in the process of hearing and receiving his communications, which may at times be quite disturbing. He needs steadiness and objectivity also with respect to the outside world from which he draws the subject matter of his curriculum. It is the business of the teacher to choose the data and truth which at the moment will help his students realize themselves in responsible relation to the world of persons and things. While it is inevitable that a teacher who is an authentic person will have a point of view and hold values that are deeply a part of his being, he must do so in such a way that they do not unduly influence the growth of his students. In fact, he will not allow himself to be crippled or destroyed by too close an identity with or conformity to a particular "party." Nor will the authentic person sell his soul for office or reputation. Whimsically, we might add that the authentic person is willing for God to occupy the heavenly throne, without a desire to take even the smallest corner of it for himself.

2. *The dialogical person is an open person,* one who is known first by his willingness and ability to reveal himself to others, and, secondly, by his willingness and ability to hear and receive their revelation. It may seem odd to use the word "revelation" in describing an open person, for it is a technical theological term primarily used to describe the activity of God. In that we are the creation of God and his revelatory action is personal, however, it seems appropriate to use the term also to describe the self-disclosing action of the human person. Then, too, the term and the action to which it points stand in sharp contrast to such terms and actions as exhibition and display suggest, although we must grant that it is often confused with these latter. Revelation does not mean making known data about oneself or exhibit-

ing powers and talents of which one is proud. Revelation means, instead, being present to another by word or action in such a way that the whole meaning and vitality of the relationship is deepened. The dialogical person does not talk about himself, but he does offer out of himself meaning to which his fellows may make free response. And to do this, he has to assume certain risks of communication and, therefore, of creativity.

These risks are real. A child, for example, may discover that what he offers is not appreciated. Or again, he may find that it is misunderstood, distorted, even scorned. And always there is the chance that it may be simply ignored. These risks of communication are very great and many people are afraid to undertake them. I find, for example, that in group discussions it is common for people to withhold contributing to a discussion either because they are afraid their comments will not be appreciated or because they fear to reveal their total selves—in other words, to be "found out." Afterwards, however, they confess that because they were afraid and refused to speak they experienced frustration, upset—a diminishment of being.

The risks of communication are experienced in still another way. I have watched a person, after making his contribution with passionate conviction, anxiously scan the group to see how his contribution is being received. Sometimes there is no comment and the contribution falls to the floor with a thud. Or again, the contribution may be distorted or misinterpreted with the result that a wave of indignation floods the contributor's soul. The open person knows these risks and is even frightened by them at times. But, nonetheless, he accepts them courageously and is thankful when genuine communication does take place. Above all, he accepts the response of others, whatever it may be, as important for the whole learning process in communication.

A person creatively participating in dialogue is one who has convictions, but they are convictions that genuinely relate to his basic character. He is also one who recognizes and accepts the convictions of others, indeed invites them to reveal them. All of us need the experience of living with people who speak out of the depths of their beliefs and stand for them with courage. One needs to accept the challenge of another's thought or questions and come to terms with the boundaries and limitations that other people's points of view impose upon him. Such a person is a growing person who helps others grow with him. Indeed, we all gain power as persons when, in dialogue with others, we state our convictions, and they, in turn, challenge or affirm us. Unfortunately, many people are afraid of this kind of revelation. Some teachers, for example, live within the limitations of academically restricted subject matter and lose all sense of the dialogical possibility of wrestling with the truth. We need ministers also who are not afraid to stand for something and yet are open to correction and growth. Too many ministers and teachers reveal a need to be right, a need that keeps them from hearing what their fellow says, which in many instances may be the truth they *really* need to hear. Laymen often state that their ministers do not like to be questioned or challenged and that for this reason they do not feel free to enter into dialogue with them. The lack of dialogue between clergy and laity weakens the Church's witness in the world. The Word of God needs to be kept in dialogue with the word of man in order that its truth may be recognized in relation to the questions for which it was given. Whenever the Church loses its capacity for dialogue with contemporary thought and culture, it becomes opinionated in its views of the world, dogmatic in its understanding and statement of the faith, and irrelevant in its teaching. The Church must never lose its power to maintain dialogue openly and undefensively with other points of view.

Not only do open persons have an ability to reveal themselves to others, but they are able to hear and receive the personal revelation of others. It is all too easy for each of us to assume that only we are the vehicle of the truth and that only through us does God speak. It is good to be reminded that he can speak to us through others and that what we should say in dialogue can be called forth by the question or comment of others. In dialogical communication the hearer is as important as the speaker. Have we not all realized that we are better able to speak in response to an individual or group that is attentive than to one that is not? Hearing is an essential part of the communication process. Some people by their indifferent manner inhibit our ability to express ourselves, and others by their attentiveness and interest help us to express ourselves with an uncommon skill and grace. The hearer has power not only to call forth and enable the speaker, and thus increase the communication, but to minister to the loneliness of the speaker as well. The act of communicating at times can be a lonely one, especially when the communication is one of challenge, involving risk and calling for courage. This can be true, for instance, in preaching. How sad it is that so few congregations are aware that their listening can play an enabling and strengthening part in the communication that is called the "sermon."

The loneliness of many preachers is an indication that the sermon is monological and that the preacher is not met by a congregation which knows itself as a partner in the act of communication. The hearer, by demonstrating that he hears and understands the speaker, meets him in the risk of communication. Such a hearer ministers to the loneliness of the communicator and joins him again to the human race.

The responsibility to listen and hear is, however, a mutual one. The parent as well as the child, the teacher as well as the student, the preacher as well as the congregation, must be ready to hear. Indeed, any fellowship should be a fellowship of hearers as well as one of speakers, a fellowship whose hearing releases people from the prisons of their prejudices, defenses, and false images of one another. All of these things—prejudices, defenses, and images—as we have seen, are ways in which we undertake to protect ourselves when we are feeling vulnerable. Dialogical communication is the medicine for the loneliness that results from human alienation and separation.

The dialogical person must also be open to the meaning and influence of the dialogue itself. The act of dialogue is one by which a person makes himself available to and aware of others, and an important part of that relationship is the meaning of what each says to the other. The concern in dialogue, therefore, is not only for persons that they may find and affirm one another, but for the meaning of the conversation between them. The content of communication is a relevant part of the relationship. When two people are trying to overcome an estrangement, the subject matter of their intercourse is both a reflection of their estrangement and a point of focus for their attempted reconciliation. The subject matter is a formulation about the relationship to which each contributes out of whatever responsibility he can muster. In other words, dialogue requires a disciplined attention to and acceptance of the content of the exchange and its meaning. Many people draw back from it because its meaning is painful and disturbing. They would like to have the benefits of relationship without its cost.

The meaning of the dialogue comes, therefore, from a twofold source: both from the participation of the persons involved and from the subject of their communication. In dialogue the open person is able to listen deeply to both sources of meaning. He has the capacity to participate in the meaning of another's life and experience. When a student, for example, heatedly rejects a teaching that challenges him, the teacher may either react emotionally and defensively in an attempt to justify himself and his point of view; or he may try to understand and participate in the meaning of the student's experience by recognizing and accepting the student's response as a legitimate element in the dialogue, and thus a part of the subject matter of the curriculum for which he, the teacher, is responsible. In the latter case, the teacher is participating in the very meaning of the student's life, and he does so by concerning himself with the experience out of which the student's communication emerged. He listens for the question behind the question, for the fear behind the bravado, for the insecurity behind the pretense, and for the courage behind the timidity, all of this being an essential part of the content of the dialogue.

Mutuality, however, is a necessary element in participation. If the teacher is to participate in the meaning of a student's life, or the minister in that of his parishioner's, then student and parishioner must also be allowed to participate in the meaning of the teacher's or minister's life. The same is true for parent and child and every other relationship. Many of us are lonely because we cannot accept the participation of others in the meaning of our lives, especially if we are in a parental or other kind of authoritative role. Recently a perceptive couple, quite concerned about the state of the clergy, observed that many clergymen seem to live lonely lives in the Church because they are unwilling to be ministered to as well as to minister. When I asked ministers of different denominations about this, many admitted its truth in their own cases. The answer to the problem is that the minister as well as the layman should each accept as his primary role that of being a member of the Church, in which person meets person and the ministry of each is available to the other. In every relationship each participant must expect to be known as well as to know.

Only in this kind of relationship is it possible for us to teach one another. According to Martin Buber, the educator himself—be he professional or amateur—meets, draws out, and forms the pupil. He prepares himself for this meeting by making himself a disciplined master of some part of man's environment. And from this he selects, from moment to moment, some element which he feels is relevant to the student's consideration at the time. This we know to be the content of the course. But the teacher stands in peril of letting this be the whole course and of mistaking the transmission of it as the full dimension of education. The purpose of education is not simply the transmission of information but the bringing into being of persons of responsibility and integrity who, in a world of persons and things, can be instruments of a love which, in the words of Paul Tillich, "moves everything toward everything else that is." The educator's responsibility is to recognize that each single unique person is the bearer of a special task of being which can be fulfilled through him and him alone.

Thus the dialogical teacher or minister is one who is free to reveal himself, to accept the revelations of others, and is open to the meaning of the dialogue between them.

3. *The dialogical person is a disciplined person.* A disciplined person is one who is able to assume responsibility for himself and others, and accepts the limitations as well as the opportunities the relationship offers. Here is a quality that is indispensable to parents, partners in marriage, teachers and ministers, and all leaders of men. Because of the privileges of communicating, we face the enormous temptation of talking too much, of allowing our verbal activity to grow without benefit of pruning. It is easy for us to reach a point in life where we assume that because we have chosen to say something it should be said, or that because we have done something it should be done. It is equally true, on the other hand, that we sometimes refrain from saying what needs to be said and from doing what needs to be done. And here we fail to speak and act because we are afraid.

There are, therefore two disciplines to be observed. The first is the discipline of giving oneself in dialogue. It is imperative that we assume the responsibility for speaking when the word needs to be spoken, for acting when the action is called for, regardless of the risks involved or how we fare in the process.

We must also accept the discipline of making our contribution in the context of the contribution of others. This means accepting our dependence upon them and repudiating the "prima donna" role that many of us find so attractive. Likewise, in the area of study one reason for many people not reading more than they do is that their thinking is disturbed by the thoughts they encounter in books. Dialogical thinking requires courage and strength of character and considerable maturity. It means giving ourselves to the truth and letting come what may. It is truly a giving of ourselves in the broadest sense. To do this means that we need to discipline our self-centeredness.

The dialogical person must be prepared to participate in the discipline of great dialogue, out of which true creativity is born. Have we not all had the experience of finally submitting our question or thought to a group of peers and then seeing emerge from the painful yet exciting wrestling with the truth an insight or understanding that was greater and more profound than that offered by any single contributor? So tremendous is this experience that we find it easy to believe that God was in the midst and that through our dialogue he made us participants in his revelations. Such an event is measured in terms both of the content produced and of the relationship experienced. That meeting between person and person, that appearance of understanding, would not have occurred, however, if the participants had not been willing to submit to the discipline of great dialogue. As we listen to the councils of churches, we are forced to conclude sometimes that dialogical encounter does not occur as frequently as it might. Instead, we find the members of the Body of Christ aggressively seeking to impose their views and prejudices on others, oblivious to the possibility that there is anything for them to hear and consider. The effect on the Church and the world is alienating and impoverishing. A man from a part of the world that had been an object of missionary activity by one of the Western denominations complained that the missionaries had imposed the Western form of Christianity on his people, even insisting on the use of English, Western clothing, and customs. "We [Christians] are now like foreigners in our own land," he said. How much more creative the situation would have become had there been dialogue between the missionaries and their traditions, and the values and customs found in the culture of the country. Out of the encounter would have come benefits to both the natives and the missionaries, and a new Church expressing its own uniqueness.

Sometimes we refrain from participation in dialogue because we are afraid that those things that need to take place will not occur, and we try to force their occurrence. At times like that we need to practice the discipline of giving ourselves, of taking the risk in spite of our fears. Be courageous, speak, and let the word and action go. They may call forth a response that will produce surprising and enabling resources for the accomplishment of an even better purpose. The result of what we say is not entirely our responsibility. It is ours only to speak our words as responsibly as possible and to submit, therefore, to the discipline of speaking and giving oneself.

A second discipline to be observed by the dialogical person is to hold oneself to one's own part and leave others free to respond and initiate as they will. One of the obstacles to communication is the tendency we have to carry on both sides of a dialogue. All of us, by drawing conclusions in advance or making assumptions about the other person's response, plan our communication to anticipate these. Such communication is not dialogue but calculated monologue, which certainly precludes our speaking freely and robs the other person of his freedom to respond.

Communication thus falls into what might be called an image impasse, and this is serious because the preconception gobbles up the meaning which might otherwise bring the participants together. Image communication is separating and alienating. Our images of each other are often insulting because they do not do justice to what the other is. Image communication depreciates, belittles, and offends us. All about us we hear people making assumptions about each other and then allowing these assumptions to determine what they say or do not say. In marriage, for example, one partner or the other, or both, may formulate their conversation on the basis of assumptions they are making about each other with the result that all communication between them is filtered through their images and is, therefore, distorted and alienating.

When people are challenged about this matter of carrying on both sides of the dialogue, their response is often that they are afraid to leave the other person free for fear of what he may say. Why should we fear more the free response of another person than the horrible distortions that grow out of clinging to our false preconceptions of them and their responses? Nothing can be any worse than the alienation that results from image encounter, especially when we realize that it has no future and can only deteriorate further.

Let us, therefore, in speaking and acting, practice the discipline of waiting for the response, and then engage with it as honestly as we can. This might be the beginning of a process that would work miracles in our relationships. I have seen couples break through this kind of image impasse and say after true communication with each other had been accomplished, "I never knew, I didn't know you were like this; I didn't know that you thought this way; I never knew how you felt." Similarly, the student needs to know the teacher as he really is, and the teacher needs to know the student as he is. Both need to communicate with one another for their own sakes and for the sake of their respective responsibilities as student or teacher, without false image distortion.

4. *The dialogical person is a related person.* By this we mean that he responds to others and is, therefore, responsible. We cannot be individuals going our separate ways. We are tied to each other and dependent on one another. The structures of human relationship are necessary for our individual lives, and we are also responsible for the maintenance of these structures. Sometimes we are tempted to resent this fact and try to be unreasonably independent, but such resentment only separates us and impairs our communication. One hears people say, "I want to be my own person; I don't want to be dependent upon or beholden to another. I resent the obligations that seem to be mine when I accept the relatedness of which you speak." And so we hold one another off. The teacher holds off the student, the minister stiff-arms the parishioner, the husband escapes from his wife by fleeing to his business, and the wife breaks the relationship and, therefore, her heart by officious preoccupation with the details of life. Relationships fall apart and communication becomes only an idea when basic relatedness is not accepted as necessary to life and love.

Therefore, if persons do not accept each other in the structures of relationship, there can be no dialogue. But it is in dialogue that acceptance is given and received. The word spoken in dialogue is an act of faith done in spite of the doubt that it will do any good. The dialogical word is an open word, a word of beginnings, because it is a word of expectation inviting response. In speaking the word of dialogue a person puts himself on the threshold of truth and becomes the servant of God. Faithfulness, therefore, to the call of God is to be measured not in terms of the propositions of belief, but in terms of willingness to give ourselves to one another, and in that giving to be open to his working through us to one another.

It is imperative, then, that a Christian be a dialogical person through whom the Word that gives life is spoken.

6 The Dialogical Crisis

Crisis in dialogue occurs when the participants—whoever they may be: teacher and student, minister and parishioner, husband and wife, parent and child—fail really to address and respond to each other but turn away defensively, each within himself, for the purposes of self-justification. Self-affirmation now takes the place of being affirmed by another in relationship, a process that produces only increasing anxiety and alienation. Our life situation is one in which we are always seeking affirmation, and if we do not receive it, we try to provide it for ourselves.

The Tragedy of Interrupted Dialogue

There exists within all of us an inner battle between the forces which affirm us and the forces that would destroy us.

All experiences of love and everything that contributes to our sense of the meaning and unity of life strengthen us, and all experiences that produce in us a sense of our finiteness, guilt, and purposelessness diminish our sense of being. Each of us, intent on achieving what he believes to be his own fulfillment, faces the temptation of using others as a quick means of reassurance and affirmation rather than receiving it through honest give-and-take. This exploitation of others, however, is always self-defeating and self-destroying, and in such a conflict both participants lose.

Examples of such exploitation are numerous: the student's desire to show up the teacher or the teacher's desire to put the student in his place, either being an instance of the desire to downgrade the other in order to upgrade himself. There is temptation on the part of the employee to exploit his relationship with his employer in order to accomplish some personal end, such as advancement or political advantage. The employer may exploit the employee in order to reinforce his own self-regard, to justify himself as a person, or to increase his reputation. Fear of losing love may cause a wife to make excessive demands for affection on her husband, and guilt may cause him to blame her excessively for some fault. In seeking to gain our own lives, however, we lose them in the end, because no matter how much we may be able to get others to do for us, something important has been lost. Can we identify this loss?

1. The first and obvious observation to make is that in these exploitive and self-justifying situations the relationship necessary for dialogue is broken because mutual trust no longer exists between the parties. Each now has to be on guard against the other; each has, in reality, become the

enemy of the other. Whatever is communicated has to be calculated. One has to weigh one's words, not in the interests of wisdom, but for the sake of safety. And when the dialogue is thus interrupted, the very interruption deepens the mutual mistrust. One's grasp on truth becomes a mere weapon with which to fight the other rather than a complementary source of wisdom capable of challenging and reuniting the participants. In time the broken, disrupted relationship may be abandoned, so that while with his lips one speaks about the fellowship and God, in his life he denies that such a relationship exists. When relationship is thus disrupted between a minister and his people, for example, the minister becomes, as it were, a mere scribe and Pharisee, and is no longer a teacher who, out of the spirit of Christ, speaks as a man having authority—in other words, as a man in authentic relation.

2. A second observation to be made on interrupted dialogue is that the person who is the victim in this broken and abandoned relationship dies. We said earlier that a person comes into being only in relation. Therefore, it is not a surprising conclusion that when the relationship is broken and abandoned, the person as person dies. This impression is confirmed when we visit a mental hospital and see there people who have been so severely hurt in the milieu of relationship that they have withdrawn from it altogether. The lifeless expressions on their faces indicate clearly that the spark of personhood has disappeared. Similarly, although often less acutely, this can happen to anyone. Students, for example, often express a deep desire to enter the dialogue of study and learning, but find that they are incapable of doing so because a gap exists between their intention and

their power of self-commitment. And this is understandable, for intention involves only the intellectual man, whereas commitment demands action of the whole man. And it is precisely the whole man who is not available for the enterprise because the student does not trust: he does not trust himself, he does not trust the teacher, he does not trust the relationship which is necessary to learning. In fact, he shows some of the symptoms of an individual who is dying as a person: he is apathetic or cynical, hostile, envious, destructively competitive, and unorganized. He may talk much about personal religion and rules of life, love to go on retreats and buy new books of prayer, but he is neither able nor ready to practice the devotion of self-giving, concentration, and affirmation. He shows a tendency to seek the formal and avoid the vital, even to substitute form for vitality, because slavery to form is the last hope of the person alienated from vitality. Certain kinds of so-called education can interrupt the dialogue and destroy the person's creativity. Dialogical education, however, can produce men in whom incentive and creative capacity are renewed.

3. The third tragedy that attends interrupted dialogue as a natural consequence of broken relationship and death of the person is the loss of God. God is dead. He is not really, of course; but to the monological person who, like the Pharisee stands "praying thus with himself," God seems to be dead. Life is no longer rich in possibility; now it is only a formulation wrapped up in habit and stored in the closet of religion. Indeed, God always seems to us to be dead when we substitute our thoughts about him for living in response to him. Martin Buber has asserted that God alone is the Being who may properly be addressed and not ex-

pressed. Our own conversations when examined, however, seem to imply that *we* discover him, *we* defend him, *we* protect him from misrepresentation, *we* undertake to bring him into this or that human situation, *we* instruct men about him—all of which suggests that if God is not dead, he is actually rather feeble. A favorite resolve is that we will make God and his Christianity relevant, as though we could make God relevant if he were not, or make him present in a situation if he were not there already. Something is wrong with our teaching and with our lives when our language unconsciously expresses this kind of belief. And something is wrong with our teaching and with our lives when church people can be so enormously preoccupied, in the name of Christ, with forms, formulations, and moralities that do not point to anything beyond themselves.

The Dynamics of Dialogical Crisis

Having seen the indispensability of relationship in dialogue for the reunion of life with life and of men with God, and having identified some of the tragedies that attend upon interrupted dialogue, let us now examine some of the forces that cause dialogical crisis. We can probably examine these best if we take a specific instance. Although the incident we are to examine is about a teacher-student relationship, the elements of it are easily relatable to other relationships: marital, parental, industrial, political, and others. Some readers may find themselves thinking in terms of these others rather than in terms of the one we are using.

The episode we are about to consider was one involving six students during, and after, the clinical pastoral training period in the summer between their first and second years at a seminary. The training program was held in a mental hospital for twelve weeks, under the direction of a chaplain-supervisor with the assistance of selected members of the hospital staff. Its purpose was to provide the students with an experience of working with people who were in some distress in order that the students might learn about persons and about their own capacity to relate to and work with them. All but one student were married, and all were candidates for the ministry. In the course of the summer's training many of the presuppositions that they had brought with them to the ministry had been challenged, and their personal adequacy for the responsibilities of the ministry had been questioned. And this despite the fact that they were reasonably attractive, able, and well-trained men who would normally be accepted for any responsible work. The reports of the supervising chaplain, however, indicated that although they showed promise and had participated in the hospital training program with enthusiasm, they had resisted antagonistically any attempt to interpret this experience in terms of their readiness for pastoral work. Several of them showed marked resistance to the attempt to get them to think through the theology that they brought to their training, in terms of the human situations with which they were dealing. When such a correlation was proposed, they looked upon it as an attempt on the part of the supervisor to "humanize" their theology.

Shortly after the opening of the fall term, these students asked the chairman of the seminary Pastoral Department in which this pastoral training was a required course, for a conference because they had some serious criticisms to make of the summer course, and of the whole curriculum of the department. When the appointed evening came, they stated that the course they had just completed was not sufficiently oriented to the purposes of the ministry and too closely related to the practice of psychiatry. They were of the opinion that the supervisor who had been in charge of their training was singularly insensitive to them and their needs. They thought that the scheduling of the course had been wrong, that it should have been offered to them later when they would be more adequately prepared for it. They were of the opinion that while the head of the department was well-intentioned, he was making serious mistakes in departmental policy and curriculum program. Both the faculty and trustees should, in their judgment, reconsider the place and purpose of this department in the seminary's curriculum. It was obvious, as these men talked, that they were under considerable emotional pressure to make these points. Their teacher's impression was that they were anxious and threatened not only by what they had been through during the past summer, but also by the present conversation.

Obviously, something was at stake here, but what was it? The basic question was not, as they had suggested, the seminary curriculum, but themselves, their security in the face of the anxieties raised by a disturbing experience. These men had entered their training for the ministry as persons who had achieved in their lives a certain organized system of security and defense; they had assumptions they believed to be true, and purposes which motivated their lives. In the course of the summer they had had encounters that made it necessary for them to examine all these, to question them, and to face the possibility that their very lives needed restructuring. This is always a disturbing prospect, and naturally they were disposed to fight against it. On the other hand, it was clear that some truth was seeping in on them. It was becoming apparent to them, for example, that they were not ready for the ministry; that as they were at present, they were not necessarily the kind of people who could help others; that their understanding of life and of the relations between men, and between men and God, were not as mature and basic as they had thought. While they wanted to hold on to what they had, they were also looking wonderingly at that which was being revealed to them. What should they choose to do? Should they cling to the old? Should they reach out and respond to the new in the faith that, perhaps, those to whom they had committed themselves for their education might know something about what they were doing? How best could they become the persons they were meant to be? How best could they actualize or affirm themselves?

They were not alone in this plight, for the one to whom they were speaking, their teacher, was in the same human predicament. He, like all teachers, was trying to affirm himself through his very function as a teacher. He, too, was trying to find his way as a person. He had convictions in response to which he had made commitments in matters of educational policy and practice, and these had deep personal meaning for him. Indeed, his very existence as a self-respecting person was, in large part, dependent upon how he realized himself as a teacher.

The process of affirmation, then, is not one that takes place casually. It is a life and death matter, and it calls for decisions about life and how it is to be lived. It is the point where one decides whether to live dialogically or to withdraw into this or that capsule of existence and, from the protection of that seclusion, let life surge with its challenges on the outside.

Each party to the dialogue under consideration felt the other as a threat to his being. The teacher-department head was both the symbol and the source of the forces opposing the motives, purposes, and structures to which the students were clinging and from which they would not voluntarily be separated. But this conflict was far from being simply an externalized one, for these students felt emerging within themselves forces which were in opposition to their old ways of life. Of these their teacher was also a symbol, for he represented that part of them that sought to be released from old forms and looked to be baptized with new vitality. The students, therefore, saw the teacher both as an enemy and a friend, a familiar enemy and a strange friend. At the moment, for the most part, they wanted him as a familiar enemy, although quite secretly they wanted him at the same time as a friend who might become less strange. On the one hand, they wanted to shut him out. On the other, they wanted him to come in and help them do that which, by themselves, they did not have the courage or ability to do.

In a similar fashion the students were a threat to their teacher. Out of their immaturity and ignorance they were challenging him, his convictions, and his commitments. They were telling him quite frankly that he was on the wrong track. Indeed, they were probably activating the very doubts he had about himself. They threatened to appeal to the authorities, the faculty, and the trustees with whom he already had some difficulty. Moreover, they were a threat to the prestige he enjoyed with other students who, without these ring-leaders, were not likely to raise the same disturbing questions. Their very questions, however, constituted a real part of the curriculum, and if he could accept them, these questions would give him his greatest teaching opportunity. In other words, they not only threatened to destroy him as teacher, but also were offering him opportunities for greatness in that role.

From this analysis we may conclude that a dialogical crisis arises from forces in conflict between the participants and is complicated by the contending, unacknowledged forces which are operating in each participant. In such a situation the possibilities of creative action are enormous, but the possibilities of withdrawal from, or abandonment of, potential transformation are very definitely present also. When we raise the question, "How should the issue be decided?" we have to reckon with a powerful need that operates in both protagonists—the need to save himself, or more theologically, the need to justify himself. Indeed, this need of individuals to be right is so great that they are willing to sacrifice themselves, their relationships, and even love for it. This need to be right is also one which produces hostility and cruelty, and causes people to say things that shut them off from communication with both God and man.

These students would have liked to vindicate themselves, to demonstrate that true education does not call for self-transformation, that its objectives can be accomplished by the mere assimilation of the propositional forms of truth, and that the themes of death and resurrection are for verbal dissemination, not for personal assimilation. That they might have had to suffer later had they been proven right was not at the moment important, for they were ready to accept any loss in order to be right. Likewise, the teacher, on his side, wanted to be vindicated and wanted to justify himself as a teacher. He was tempted, because he was human, to choose his cause, his philosophy of education, his technique of procedure, instead of the students and their need of help. He felt a need to play it safe, to keep in harmony with "the powers that be," to honor the form of truth even though his practice belied it.

Accordingly, implicit in this need to save oneself is the corresponding need to sacrifice the other. In order to save himself the student must sacrifice the teacher: he must exploit him, persecute, misrepresent, or distort him. And to do this he also stands ready to sacrifice the school, what it stands for, and what it is trying to do. Indeed, when such is the case not even the ministry of the Church, the truth, or even God himself stand outside the student's destructive path. All this the student is willing to sacrifice, throw away, discard, ignore, and trample on in order to justify himself.

In the dialogue we are reporting and analyzing, the students came perilously close to telling the teacher that so far as they were concerned, he could "go to hell." And he, on his part, was tempted to sacrifice them. He wanted to choose himself, his curriculum, his objectives, and his methods over against the students, their needs, their education, and his responsibility as an instrument of God's salvation for them. At best, we must say that his deepest desire was that they accept him and his need, and conform to his thought and way.

Another element operating in the dynamics of dialogical crisis is the appeal of truth, an appeal which, of course, exerts great pressure on the partners in dialogue if they do not shut themselves off from its influence. A spirit of truth is in every true dialogue and acts through and between the participants.

When the teacher and students later evaluated their conflict, they both acknowledged a sense of this spirit, during the crisis, that was both within and beyond themselves. This presence seemed to be on the side of courage and freedom, and both students and teacher acknowledged that in the course of their conflict it was possible for them to be either open or closed to the truth's presence and work. This presence seemed to be concerned not only with the state of the relationship between the two parties, but also with the meaning of the content of the relationship. They felt that their attention was being drawn to the significance of what was happening between them as a part of the curriculum, and to the meanings that others were bringing to the controversy. As a result of the dialogue each participant was being helped to rise above his self-centered concern and to find a point of meeting in which the meaning of content and the meaning of persons complemented one another. Truth was liberating them from fears and defenses and giving them courage to be.

We can sum up the analysis we have been making by restating the five elements in a dialogical crisis: (1) the drive on the part of each to affirm himself; (2) the threat that each feels in the other with respect to the accomplishment of that goal; (3) the need on the part of each to save and justify himself; (4) the need on the part of each to sacrifice the other in order to save himself; and (5) the participation in this crisis of the spirit of truth whose purpose is to move everything to everything else that is.

We all find ourselves in this human predicament whenever real communication is either about to take place or to be abandoned. It happens whenever there is a crisis that calls for decision on the part of someone; and it is a crisis that is repeated again and again in the course of everyone's life. We can say either Yes or No to the possibility of real communication, although the more we say No, the less likely are the possibilities of its occurring. The real tragedy and pathos of the human situation is that we can say No so often that we become deaf and dumb to all further appeals; but because we still go through the motions of hearing and speaking, we continue to assume that we are in communication with God and man, though in reality we are living by the forms of life only. Many ministers who come to the Institute confess that they are concerned because when they speak they do not say anything, and when they listen they do not seem to hear anything. Because the possibilities and perils of communication are so great, we naturally ask the question: Who shall deliver us from deafness and dumbness? How shall the issue be determined on the side of dialogue? The New Testament tells us very simply that Christ made the dumb speak and the deaf hear. We all want this miracle, this miracle of dialogue, to happen to us.

Courage to Resume a Dialogue

Some help is needed if we are to assume the creative risk to continue or resume our part in a dialogue which is in crisis. When we hear someone discussing the possibility of resuming communication, we get the impression that what is needed for the undertaking is courage, courage to stick one's neck out, courage to take the initiative, courage to make an offering that may not be accepted, courage to endure being ignored or misrepresented if that should be the response. Furthermore, we know from observation that when a person has this courage and acts on it, he experiences a feeling of liberation. Our own observation, then, seems to give us the first clue to the answer, namely, that courage is necessary if dialogue is to take place.

The second clue comes from the Scriptures where we read in the first chapter of the second Epistle to Timothy: "The Lord did not give us the spirit of timidity, but the spirit of power, love, and self-control." The answer to the timidity that keeps us from daring the risks of communication lies in our using all the power we can muster to be really present to others, in love that enables us to stand with them and try to see life from their point of view, and in the discipline that controls our temptation to try short-cuts to security and affirmation.

The principle underlying dialogue is: "He who loses his life for my sake and the Gospel shall find it." This means that we enter into relationship not for the purpose of gaining, but for the purpose of giving, with the prayer that we may lose our pretentions, our defensive need to justify ourselves, and gain, instead, a reassurance of life by having it affirmed in our relationship with another.

The importance of courage in dialogue deserves extended consideration. And while the specific instance of it we are discussing is taken from teaching, all that we are saying about it is equally applicable to every situation in which dialogue is possible.

In dialogue someone has to take the initiative. In the case we were discussing, the teacher had to embody for his students the acceptance he had experienced and, out of his own reassured existence, to affirm the existence of his students. He had to provide them with a pattern of fearlessness which, in turn, evoked in them courage to face the perils of learning and growing. The students, however, really took the initiative, by arranging the meeting with him for the purpose of raising questions that would challenge him. This took courage because while they were threatened by him, they were also dependent upon him. There may have been some prior quality in his relation to his students that helped them have the courage to speak.

In any event, the concern of the educator is not with what happens to him as a teacher, but with what he can do for the students. He knows, in the first place, that real becoming takes place through the encounter of person with person, and that he may be one such nurturing person for his students. Therefore, he must be one who is willing to assume responsibility for them while, at the same time, helping them grow in responsibility for themselves. The teacher knows that access to his students comes through winning their confidence.

The seminarians had been reassured when they felt that their teacher "accepted them before trying to influence them," which freed them to ask their questions. Their part of the discussion revealed that they were trusting him and, because they trusted him they were better able to accept the pain of changing and being educated. One of the first tasks of the teacher, therefore, is to awaken the trust of the learner in order that the process of learning may begin to take place.

There is another aspect of education that is commonly

overlooked, and yet is important to the teaching relationship. We observe that learning is often blocked because a pupil is alienated from himself, from others, including the teacher, and from the truth he is seeking to learn. Signs of his alienation are seen in his hostility, passivity, inattention, or distraction. These states of alienation obstruct the process of teaching and learning. The teacher, too, brings similar difficulties to the teaching relationship, but because he is the teacher and, therefore, responsible, it is expected of him that he will have gained some power of insight and self-acceptance through his own sense of being accepted and will be able, therefore, to accept the effects of his student's alienation. He will not allow the symptoms of his student's alienation to stand between and separate them. Instead of reacting to the symptoms, he will try to break through them and person-to-person speak to his students, meeting them in their loneliness, and thus awakening in them that trust without which neither teaching nor learning may take place. We may call this aspect of education the reconciling work of the teacher. This is how education participates in saving action.

There is more, however, to the process: the acceptance of death as a necessary prelude to new life, symbolized by the Crucifixion. When students begin to ask their real questions, when they begin to employ their new autonomy as thinking and acting persons in relation to the autonomous oppositeness of their teacher, and when they experience the pain of learning, conflict must result. Here the teacher meets his supreme test! He must be true to himself as a person, to his values, and to his responsibility for his students. He dare not destroy the honesty of the dialogue between himself and his students by compromise, and yet he must not allow the relationship to degenerate into a battle of wills! The teacher must accept, with the word of love, the actions and responses of the students, no matter how emotional and defensive they may be. He must look upon them as making a painful pilgrimage.

In this way the teacher keeps open the relationship while he still speaks as an authority out of his insights and values. This is a painful task and teachers shrink from it! But this kind of encounter, difficult as it is, often provides teachers with their greatest educational opportunities. Everything that passes between students and teachers may be educative because "it is not the educational intention but the meeting which is educationally fruitful." (Martin Buber, *Between Man and Man*) Teachers can look back upon many educational experiences with students which, at the time, seemed to be most unpromising, if not destructive. Yet as time went on and the seed that was planted had opportunity to grow, many of these relationships proved to be the kind in which reconciliation and transformation occurred.

In the context of this kind of teaching, the intellectual instruction becomes really important and profoundly significant. The meaning of the content meets the meaning which the students bring out of their lives to this moment of learning, and the meeting is made possible through the integrity of the relationship provided by the teacher.

There is no doubt that the teacher's task is enormous, but it is possible when the teacher embodies for his students the acceptance of Christ, that is, when he brings into play his own faith in order to awaken the trust of his students. The teacher does not do the work of redemption out of his own power, because the teacher himself is in need of the same redemption as that of his students. The teacher himself must first be saved from the forces that would destroy him as a teacher, and only then can he hope to be the instrument of salvation for his students.

Courage, Dialogue, and the Church

Thus far we have considered only the personal dimension in dialogical crisis, a dimension that underlies all crises and is, in some ways, the easier to describe and understand. During the past fifty years, many discoveries and insights have focused on the area of personal and group relations. It should not be surprising, therefore, that education, religion, and community agencies of various kinds have also been primarily concerned with personal and family life. At the same time the industrial revolution and the advance of science have confronted us with great, complex, social, economic, and political problems. Our educational, religious, and civic institutions have been criticized for being concerned with personal and family life at the expense of concern for these great social issues. Indeed, critics are not backward in pointing out that leadership on the frontiers of human existence is provided, in many instances, by people who regard the Church as obsolete and irrelevant. Moreover, the attempts to arouse in church people a responsibility to witness in these areas in the name of Christ often produce disappointing results. A church will not assume responsibility for the world when it is not living dialogically with the world, when it does not see itself as the voice of the Spirit in re-creating exchange with the world. In other words, the defensive image that many church members have of the Church as the safety deposit box in which spiritual valuables are kept, needs to be changed to an image of it as the incarnation of the spirit of the Master. When a Christian really serves the Lord of truth, he will have a forward, not a backward look. Instead of cluttering men's minds and spirits with the relics of past religious life, whether a hank of hair, an unthought-out theological proposition, or a dated moralism, he will engage contemporary men in conversation about the things that seem important to them and help them to see the ultimate truth and values beyond the ones they now hold. And the new image of the Church must include a view of itself being informed, corrected, and purified by its dialogue with the world because we know that the Spirit judges and re-creates it, and sometimes does so through men who acknowledge no allegiance to our Lord and who are unaware of his presence and work.

If Christians would be like Christ, they must expect to become dialogical persons to and through whom he may speak. The incarnation in us of the spirit of dialogue would cleanse the Church of the sickness of clericalism and parochialism, and prepare the Church in its dispersed life for participation in God's saving work in the world. Devotion to the causes of God are a natural fruit of the spirit of dialogue, but, lacking that spirit, it is natural for the Church to love itself and be oblivious to the purpose of its existence. Those who stoutly maintain the *status quo* are obviously concerned for themselves only and find it impossible to act in behalf of racial justice or Church unity. Appeals to them only stiffen their resistance. We need to beware of monological groups that separate man from man by fostering hatred and bigotry, through insistence on one point of view against any other. Among them are the Birch Society and

Communism, both of which use strikingly similar methods in spite of the Birchers' claim that they exist to fight communism. Because they cannot "experience the other side," much less recognize that there is one, they cannot engage in dialogue. The miracles of dialogue are not possible to them, which means that they are not open to the truth. If men are not open to the truth, it cannot be in them. But Christian men, while repudiating fascistic doctrines and methods, must keep in dialogue with them with the hope that they may again be brought into reciprocal relation with truth.

Finally, one word of caution. The dialogical role is often misinterpreted to mean that one does not take a stand, especially a stand against what seems to be a majority. On the contrary, the dialogical role means to take a stand. Martin Luther superbly illustrated it when he declared, "Here I stand." Before his act there was no dialogue and no Reformation. His act provided polarity. His words and actions called forth a response and initiated a dialogue out of which the Word of God spoke and was heard afresh. Our own age needs a return to dialogue, and out of it God may choose to speak again.

Throughout this discussion we have attempted to emphasize that the truths which we have been pointing to are applicable to all relationships and not alone to those engaged in teaching. In every dialogical impasse someone is needed to take the initiative and exercise the courage for a possible breakthrough. In marriage it may be the husband at one time, the wife at another; or they might even act together. Not infrequently the one who takes the risk does it alone, and is acting not only for himself but for his partner, and for the relationship as well. Or it may be that an individual or a church may have to take a position and speak challengingly in some social or political crisis. I am thinking of the rector of a church outside New York City, who spoke out against the racial discrimination which characterized the policy of a country club which church members accepted and participated in. He provoked dialogue on a crucial issue where none had existed, which called the participants into a reconsideration of their values and loyalties. Such an undertaking is often lonely and seems to go unrewarded. We shy from such an ordeal, and yet the Christ who knew the loneliness and emptiness of the cross before he knew the resurrection, gives us, through his Spirit, his power, his love, his self-control for participation in the crises of dialogue.

7 The Fruits of Dialogue

W_E HAVE now examined the importance of dialogue, how it overcomes barriers, what is its purpose, what is required of those who engage in it, and what is the nature of the dialogical crisis. It remains to ask: What can we expect of dialogue? What are the fruits of dialogue?

We can expect miracles of dialogue because, as we have described it, dialogue brings us face to face with truth in a relationship of love. As each person speaks and responds honestly to the other, each moves toward the other and includes him. This kind of meeting between man and man cannot occur without an implicit meeting between man and God. To really see another is to see the Other, and to really love another is to love the Other. When we are truly known by another we are known by God, and to be truly loved by another is to know the love of God. Dialogue, as we have been thinking of it, is more than communication. It is communion in which we are mutually informed, purified, illumined, and reunited to ourselves, to one another, and God. A spirit pervades and directs the "conversation," and from this spirit, which Christians believe was fully incarnate in Christ, come the fruits of the Spirit. Dialogue is a condition and relationship for the appearance and work of his Spirit, which calls men to, and enables them for, dialogue out of which comes the fruits of dialogue, of the Spirit.

The fruits of the Spirit are not achieved in a vacuum. They are achieved and found in the context of human relationships, and, as we have seen, human relationships at their best are dialogical. We look there for the fruits of the Spirit: love, joy, peace, patience, kindness, goodness, faithfulness, gentleness, and self-control. These are the signs of the Christian life, or put another way, of a life lived in responsible, reciprocal relationship. Unfortunately, however, we are apt to think of these signs in the abstract, as achievements apart from the process which produces them. Love, for instance, is not a ready-made, easily purchased product. Indeed, we cannot understand love except as we see it striving in behalf of all its enemies. Peace accepts strife as part of its responsibility. Patience or long-suffering has meaning only in relation to the conflicts, distortions, and misrepresentations of life. Goodness is not innocence, but a quality of life that has wrestled with some of the forms of evil, indeed the very principle of evil itself. Gentleness is not weak but strong, and has been forged out of the temptation to be hostilely aggressive, to use compulsion as a way of achieving one's own will. And self-control trembles in its conflict with self-will.

When a man and a woman, for example, achieve a sense of deeper love that unites them more closely than ever, they know and can recall the conflicts, bitterness, and misunderstandings of one another through which they had to work in order to be reunited more deeply in love. Or, many a parish minister and his people have had the experience of moving through misunderstandings and turmoil in order to have the mutual respect and sense of faithfulness in relationship to one another and God that they have achieved. Likewise, as we have seen, the teacher knows that his self-control, patience, and joy in lessons learned by both him and his students emerge out of the pain and doubt that must accompany every search for truth, and for one another in the search for truth. The gifts of the spirit of truth are given in conjunction with our willingness to submit ourselves to the responsibility and discipline of dialogue.

Some Cases of Dialogue and the Work of the Spirit

Some cases may help us to recognize the fruits of dialogue as they occur in various relationships.

1. *Between person and person.* When June and Eric met, they had steeled themselves against any kind of personal involvement with other people. June, attractive, thirty-two years old and unmarried, was shy, fearful of offending others, and filled with all kinds of imprisoning assumptions about the kind of person she was. Her great fear was that in loving others, she might be seeking some advantage for herself; that she might be using others or they using her.

She had a great longing for relationships in which honesty prevailed and in which the possibility of exploitation would be eliminated. Eric, a few years older and separated from his wife, was a creative person whose powers were diminished by his cynical attitude toward human relations, an attitude which covered his intense need, frustrated until now, to love and to be loved. He, too, longed for honest personal relations but had given up the hope that they were possible for him.

In their first conversation together, which took place after a meeting in which the participants had engaged in evasion and double-talk, both June and Eric commented alike about how hard it is for people to be honest with each other. Each believed that the effort required to achieve a true and honest relationship with others, be it in families, friendship, or business, was so great that it was difficult to maintain. They agreed that it was not only hard to accept the honesty of others about themselves, but equally difficult to be honest with them. Their sharing of this concern for honesty gave them the courage to be honest with each other.

In everything that Eric said—and he spoke out of his convictions—he manifested an interest in and care for June. She responded to his interest and care with animation and an expression of her interest and affection, although as yet she did not identify this as such. When she became aware of what was happening between them and in her, she drew back into herself, fearful that Eric might be trying deliberately to change her into something that she was not. Again and again, he would have to reassure her that she was responding with herself, and that their relationship was the environment that was calling her forth as a person. Gradually, she even began to see that her concepts of herself were images constructed as a defense against being hurt in a world where relationships, according to her experience, could not be trusted. As it became evident that Eric not only liked her but loved her, she became troubled because she could not believe that anyone could care for her in that way. This experience raised questions in her mind as to whether Eric could be trusted or whether he merely found her convenient and was cultivating the relationship in order that he might use her for his own purposes.

In the early stages of their relationship these fears caused June to become depressed and to withdraw into herself. She also felt guilty, because it seemed to her that she was not able to assume all the responsibilities for Eric that she should. When she withdrew, Eric would encourage her to tell him what was bothering her. Gradually she was able to do so, and they had their first experience of dialogue. Sometimes the things that June had to say hurt Eric and complicated his own personal problems and being; but he was becoming so aware of her, and experienced so much of her side of the relationship, that he was able to break through his own anxieties and speak as a caring person to her. As she became reassured and able to accept herself because of his acceptance of her, she discovered in herself power that had been dormant, the power to minister to him and to ask him about his suffering, his questions, his doubts, indeed, to break through her own anxieties in order to reach him and strengthen his faith.

As time went on, it became apparent to both of them that their ability to deal honestly with whatever thought or feeling or incident lay between them was precious. They recognized that neither of them could solve any of their problems separately, that it was imperative that each seek the help of the other; and that the worst thing they had to fear was to let anything keep them from their relationship of dialogue. As a result, June became a stronger and more resourceful person and lost her fear of having a nervous breakdown. Instead of being cold and withdrawn, she became warm, outgoing, and affectionate. In place of her limited concept of her abilities, she acquired a sense of her potentialities for accomplishment. Her growing resources for dealing with crises, in spite of her anxieties, called forth Eric's admiration.

The effect on Eric was equally remarkable. June brought to him an unusual power to accept him in spite of his poor history in personal relations, his pessimism, and his lack of belief in himself. Many times her quiet and realistic inclusion of him for what he was in her thoughts and affections was a source of strength and confidence to him. As a result of her belief in him, he lost his cynicism and depressive outlook, which hitherto had taken the edge off his creativity. When he was discouraged and bottled up with feelings he could not express, she gently but firmly forced him to tell her his trouble, even though his response often caused her anxiety and difficulty. They learned that if they kept things to themselves, they would drift away from each other and get lost in the darkness of their fears and doubts. When this began to happen to either of them, it was up to the other to be the "search-party." June's persistence freed Eric from the destructive effects of his negative feelings and released his creative powers for love and work. Her steady expression of acceptance of and belief in him changed his attitude

toward himself, others, and life in general, so that he became more open and optimistic and acquired qualities of
understanding and patience. A deep sense of joy began to
take the place of the old melancholy, and a restored sense of
purpose began to crowd out the old sense of futility.

The power of this relationship was all the more notable
because their love was denied the natural expression of
marriage, owing to religious and family difficulties. Their
situation might have destroyed them were it not for the
spirit of love and of power and of self-discipline that was
born out of their faithful dialogue. As a consequence, they
grew in love and understanding and ability to live responsibly with each other in spite of anxieties, guilt, and frustration. And they were better able to give to others because of
what they gave to and received from each other, so that the
fruit of dialogue benefited them and the world in which they
lived as well.

2. *Between leader and group.* A young clergyman,
having recognized that his parishioners did not understand
the nature of his ministry, presented them with a carefully
prepared outline and description of his various duties, in-
dicating how he divided his time between them. He felt
somewhat apologetic about the little time he set aside for
study; but much to his amazement, he discovered that many
of the members of his board were surprised that he should
spend six hours a week studying, and expressed the opinion
that he might better use that time promoting the work of
their parish. His first reaction was one of indignation, which
kindled hostility on both sides. He recognized, however,
that if he were able to keep himself open to these men, to
deal with the meanings that they brought to the discussion,

and to accept these as part of the curriculum the situation provided, it might be possible for all to move from their present level of understanding to a deeper one.

And, indeed, this proved to be the case. The young minister subsequently reported that his parishioners had come to a new understanding of the nature of the Church, its task in the world, his role as the ordained member of the Church in relation to their role as lay members. He believed this to have been one of the best things that could have happened to his parish. It was made possible because the meanings of the pastor and those of the people met in a dialogue that renewed the relationship.

Another result of this confrontation, a fruit of this dialogue, was that the minister lost his sense of loneliness—he was no longer a leader who was not understood by his people. Apparently, this kind of loneliness is common to the situation of many clergymen. They feel that the Church's problems are their problems, and instead of sharing them with the membership and knowing the companionship of tackling problems together, they stagger around their communities with burdens on their minds and hearts they were never meant to carry. Doing this and living like this, they are illustrating the monological approach to social responsibility and can never know the liberating effect of dialogue.

3. *Between fields of knowledge.* Many students of the psychological sciences and of theology feel uneasy, unfortunately, whenever dialogue between their two disciplines is attempted. The students of the social sciences represent disciplines which raise questions about human existence to which Christianity is supposed to be an answer. They undertake to describe the nature and manner of man's living, the

predicaments in which he finds himself, and the ambiguities with which he is faced. Man's actual existence stands in sharp contrast to what seems to be his essential potentialities, and questions, therefore, emerge concerning his purpose and destiny. Without the existentialist description, such as comes from the study of man, affirmations about the nature of man's being are likely to be idealistic, and discussions about his need of salvation theoretical.

Dialogue, then, that strives to formulate a doctrine of Man is imperative, a task which must be tackled afresh by each generation. Contemporary study has given us a deeper understanding of the nature, functioning, and predicament of man, which helps us to see anew, in the terms of a descriptive science, the insights of Augustine and the Reformation. Protestantism, after the Reformation, settled for a weakened concept of the power of sin and of the reuniting power of grace, combining that weakened concept with an emphasis on individual and social morality. So pervasive has been this Pelagianism that a high percentage of church members believe that their membership in the Christian fellowship depends upon "keeping the law" and "doing good." The insights of the various disciplines studying man, however, have revealed how vain is the appeal to free will, and how empty of power the moralistic approach to human need. Their contribution has helped us to understand the radical alienation that exists between egocentric man and God who is Love. And this understanding of the radical nature of the human problem has helped us to comprehend how radical in nature should be the remedy. Understanding the questions that come out of human existence prepares us to understand the crucial and decisive answer implicit in the gospel. Without the background of these radical questions we might see the gospel answers only superficially and complacently.

The description of the unconscious and its functioning, which the psychological sciences have elaborated, has also influenced the doctrine of Man and has undermined moralism by showing that the emotional forces in human life are too strong to be directed and controlled by rational process alone. The uncovering of unconscious motivations that operate even through conscious processes makes clear to us that we cannot trust ourselves to do good. We can will the good; but that which we would do, we cannot. Even though we may keep the law in its letter, we will sin in the spirit. Something is needed to change the spirit of man in order that his behavior may be altered. Legalistic, moralistic religion has always imposed from above its standards upon people and, in so doing, failed to awaken in them a sense of personal responsibility. Therefore, under moralism, life is lived in response to the expectations of some big "they," and this closes men off from the possibility of being re-created by a new spirit which alone could produce an authentic morality in response to the new relationship. It is interesting to note that the psychological rediscovery of the nature of man and of his need in this respect coincides with the theological rediscovery of the work of the Holy Spirit and our dependence upon him.

Another insight born out of the dialogue between the social sciences and theology bears on the concept of salvation. Interpretations of man have oscillated from the view of his being totally depraved to that of his being able, of his own power, to build the kingdom of God. Neither view is a true one. Implicit in man's sickness is health, and his very estrangement and separation imply relationship, unity, and wholeness. Man's sickness and sin are to be understood not only in terms of morality but also in terms of the dynamics of his being. Sin and sickness are signs of man's attempt to find himself, to actualize himself in relation to all the forces of life that seem to threaten and prevent his self-realization. The struggle for self-actualization points in two directions: first, to that which man existentially is, and second, to what he may become. Jesus anticipated these insights: he saw man's existential plight, but he also saw something else in him on which he could build. He had the power to speak to men through their consciousness and change their unconscious motivations. He called men out of their existential plight and brought them into a creation of new possibilities.

We now know, as a result of the contributions of psychotherapy, that when we are *really* present to a distressed person and stand with him in his distress, when we hear him and accept him and his problems, help him to accept and use them as his curriculum, and allow the relationship between us to be the school in which the problems of his curriculum can be worked out, we are often able to reach and change the inner dynamics of his living from one of destruction to one of wholeness. If a man's relationship to man is changed in this way, he is changed and stands in another relationship to God.

Unfortunately, this view in depth of the potential of human nature and the possibilities for healing in dialogue is not shared by too many ministers. Because their understanding of man is superficial, their ministry to men does not reach them in the depths of their living and does not bring the human question into dialogical relation to the Divine Answer.

In this time of threatened tyranny and terrorism we need an alternative, and that alternative is dialogue. Whenever anyone holds whatever truth he has dogmatically and without openness, he is participating in tyranny and turning his back on dialogue. All men, whether they function in education, religion, industry, or the civic realm, must choose whether they are going to serve tyranny or dialogue, whether they are going to serve their own special interests or those of man and God. If they choose dialogue, their relation to truth will be open, non-excluding, and growing.

4. *Between a management and a labor group.* The necessity for dialogue between these two groups became acute as a result of the conditions created by the industrial revolution, which moved production from the home and guilds into industrial centers. The need for dialogue between those who owned and managed and those who worked had, of course, existed for centuries. The history of the exploitation of the peasant needs no elaboration here. And the description now being widely read in Irving Stone's *The Agony and Ecstasy*, of the exploitation of Michelangelo by the Church reveals how vulnerable were artists, craftsmen, and workmen. The development and concentration of industry in the last century has made even more obvious the conditions needing correction: hours of work, working conditions, seniority rights, health and safety, the right of representation, living conditions, to name only a few.

The early stages of the relationship between management and labor were marked often by intense hostility, violence, and disregard of the truth. But it was all a part of the dialogue. The famous "battle of the overpass" at the Ford Motor Company, for instance, was a part of the give-and-take that led to a new relationship in which each came to respect and deal responsibly with the other.

In an address before the Personnel Conference of the American Management Association on "The Case for Free Collective Bargaining," Earl R. Bramblett, director of Labor Relations at General Motors Corporation, identified some of the basic policies that guide the corporation in its collective bargaining relationships: First, the recognition of the importance of the individual; that labor relations on the job are regarded as relations between persons rather than as cold, contractual or impersonal relationships. Second, a full acceptance of unions as representatives of employees who have selected them. Third, a recognition of the mutuality of interest between employer and employee.

In connection with these policies Mr. Bramblett stressed the importance of meeting and communication. He said, "If we talk long enough, we will find out what the issue is, what we are fighting about, and, therefore, what we have to do. . . . It is important that each side shall be free to represent itself and each side be responsible for understanding the other, and together discuss the general economic outlook, the prospects of the automobile business, and the current status of the collective bargaining relationship between them."

When time for negotiation comes, the dialogue that has led up to it prepares them for their task: "We don't need to be introduced. We communicate in frank, plain language. There is no need for a go-between. . . . The preamble to our labor agreements over the last twenty years represents the spirit of dialogue: 'The management of General Motors recognizes that it cannot get along without labor, any more than labor can get along without management. Both are in the same business and the success of that business is vital to all concerned. This requires that both management and the employees work together . . . [realizing] that the basic interests of employers and employees are the same. However, employees and the management have different ideas on various matters affecting their relationship. . . . There is no reason why these differences cannot be peacefully and satisfactorily adjusted by sincere and patient effort on both sides.' "

Thus, the fruit of this dialogue today is to be found in the resulting improved relations between these important sections of society, upon which the welfare of our social order depends so much. But more than that is accomplished. When men, out of their respective interests, give themselves to the discipline of mutual understanding and effort, they achieve a greatness and capacity of spirit that is its own reward.

5. *Between countries.* In a seminar on United States and Soviet relationships, a participant expressed doubt about the value of the State Department's discussions with the Russians, and he suggested that we withdraw our effort until greater response was possible. The other members of the seminar were unanimous in their rejection of his proposal. And their understanding was the true one: that the only hope for the future rests in a relentless effort to keep open the lines of communication and in an acceptance of double-talk, rejection, and distortion as a part of the dialogue. The history of the relations between the United States and England illustrates what can be accomplished between nations when dialogue is maintained. Here again, we see that its content included exploitation, misunderstanding, misrepre-

sentation, anxiety, defensiveness, even war, but also that there was recognition of a common heritage, a need of each other, and a common responsibility. Persistence in dialogue and the acceptance of all that happened between us as part of that dialogue kept us together and helped forge the bonds that bind us in a relationship of trust and cooperation.

These five types of dialogue all illustrate how man may move toward man in relationships that include them both and all that happens between them, in the midst of which the fruits of the Spirit may appear. We turn now to review some basic changes that dialogue can produce.

Some Changes Produced by Dialogue

1. *Dialogue forms in us the characteristics of the dialogical person.* June and Eric did not originally have these qualities and capacities. In the early stages of their relationship, labor and management were incapable of sitting down together to work out agreements. It had been commonly assumed that religion and science were natural enemies and that dialogue between them was impossible, and yet the dialogue between them has increased and deepened because their attitudes toward each other were changing. Denominational exclusiveness and strict separation have also given way to relationships in which the possibilities of union are being explored not only between Protestant bodies but also between the Protestant and Roman Catholic churches. These changes in activity have produced changes in character and expectation, which in turn increase and deepen the dialogical activity.

The experience of dialogue gives more courage for accepting and overcoming the barriers to communication and, therefore, to relationship. Prior to their experience with each other, June and Eric were easily defeated by these barriers, even to the point of not believing that there was anything they could do about them. The experience of dialogue, however, changed them from monological to dialogical persons. Because each made an honest attempt to deal with the meanings of their relationship, each received gifts of courage and the capacity to accept pain while pursuing truth and achieving union. Their timidity was swallowed up in courage, and their defensiveness was transformed into a power to affirm and to venture further.

2. *Dialogue can change the meaning of experience.* Our experiences of suffering, disappointment, disillusionment, and conflict are changed from signs of failure and doom to occasions for possible renewal. The suffering, for example, that accompanied the exchange between the teacher and students whose case was considered in Chapter 6 was real for both. But they both learned that pain, anxiety, and doubt had to be accepted if growth, change, and learning are to take place. The experiences from which June and Eric used formerly to withdraw because of fear of pain can now be accepted by them. The pain is still real; the doubt and fear are still doubt and fear; but by accepting them, they find a strength and a fulfillment beyond them that changes their lives. Far from being evil, tension can be good and a source of creativity. After all, without tension the string of a violin or piano would not give forth a musical note.

3. *Through dialogue, life situations acquire new possibilities.* Real life—life that *is* life—is meeting, meeting between person and person. The excitement and promise of any gathering of people springs from the possibility that two or more persons, living most of the time in some degree of loneliness, will rendezvous, like two astronauts, in the infinity

of relationship, and from this meeting, move on to discover new worlds of meaning. Many of our relationships are realizations of this possibility; yet, tragically, too many of them are tombs in which the possibilities of meeting are buried. But the person, whose character and expectations have changed his capacity to speak and to leave the other free to respond, finds that what had appeared to be drab human situations have become occasions for new adventure. So far as the meaning of relationships and life is concerned, we are like prospectors for gold, walking aimlessly back and forth over the richest of lodes, without knowing the wealth that is beneath our feet.

4. *In dialogue is revealed the comprehensive, related character of truth.* Our severely limited, individual grasp of truth needs to be held forth openly for completion by being tested against other views. Real meetings between persons can accomplish this. All men have a contribution to make to human understanding and knowledge, be it ever so small, but they need an enabling environment in which to make it. That environment is dialogue, in which the meanings and resources of each call forth the meanings and resources of the other. All of us have experienced a birth of insight or growth of understanding in discussion between two or more persons that could not have been produced by any one of the discussants alone. The truth of each needs to be brought into relation with the truth of others in order that the full dimension of the truth each has may be made known. Such is the task of dialogue.

The fruit of dialogue is the reunion of man with himself, with others, and with God who is the source and revealer of all truth, and whose Spirit is free to guide only when men open themselves to him by turning honestly to one another.

8 Dialogue and the Tasks Ahead

ONE purpose of dialogue which we have identified is the restoration of the tension between vitality and form (Chapter 4). And by "vitality" we meant the "stirrings of new life." As we saw, this vitality needs to express itself in some appropriate form and, therefore, constantly seeks to renew the old form or find a new one, so that form will be responsive to and expressive of life. On the other hand, form constantly seeks to hold vitality captive. This is what happens when the expression of our individual, social, or religious life becomes formal and institutionalized. The Church's organizational needs and demands, for example, may confuse, if not obliterate, its mission. We are tempted by our *status quo* needs to deny the promptings of vitality, cling to the old forms of experience, and resist any renewal of them by a re-creating spirit. *We do not want to be disturbed!*

Our attitude toward the challenges of vitality, however, *is* mixed. Because man is a spirit, he has to become what he is, not an isolated self, but one responsive to his immediate and ultimate realities. Because he is a spirit, man is never satisfied with the form in which he finds himself. There is within him not only the need to capture and confine vitality for the sake of his security, but the need also to break out of the form which he has known and find new forms which are more adequate to his becoming. It is because of this urge toward more embracing and more responsive forms that reformations have taken place. There are moments of dialogue when the spirit of man overcomes his fear of the risks of creativity and responds to the promptings of vitality.

Vitality, however, must be tested, and the spirits must be tried to see if they be true. How does one test the nature of the vitality except through dialogue—test what one believes is true against what seems to be true in spite of the evidence sometimes that it ought not to be true. Too frequently we draw back from this kind of test. There is an untamed, undisciplined, "wild" quality about vitality that makes us uneasy and causes us to retreat back into the old and familiar. And yet, we must accept the wild quality of vitality if we would benefit from its renewing power. That quality must be expressed while it searches for its appropriate forms, and its expression must be accepted as a part of the tension. The vitality of adolescence in all of its expressions, including the bizarre ones, must be accepted while the young person finds, or is helped to find, his own way and style of life. In training a horse, it is important not to break his spirit because it is his spirit, during and after the training period, which will determine his style and endurance. Does education, we may ask, allow for the expression of the wildness of vitality during the educational process, or does it repress vitality in the interest of form and conformity? There is evidence that all education, theological education included, stifles the creative spirit of many students and burdens them with unassimilated and uncorrelated content. The form of knowledge has been substituted for the vitality of living and thinking.

Similarly we must ask, does religion allow for the undomesticated and the unconventional responses of people to the surges of vitality and the movements of spirit? In the area of thought, for example, many graduates of seminaries are so afraid of being heretical that they are unable to think courageously and creatively. Orthodoxy is not an alternative to heresy; it is the result of honest (*ortho*—straight) thinking about truth in relation to new needs and data, in the course of which points of view have been arrived at, tested, and abandoned. The sin is not in thinking heretically while seeking the truth, but in settling for heresy as a substitute for truth. When fear of heresy prevails, the forms of system have stifled the vitality of thought.

It is hard to understand why religion and its institutions, which should be a source of renewal for life, become the servants of a sterile conservatism. Why are churches not more commonly places where, in the spirit of Christ, creative wrestling with the problems of the human situation can take place? Why are church people in both their individual and organized lives so often conformists, substituting middle class conventions and morality for the searching, disturbing truth of Christ? The Church was brought into being to be the expression of that spirit in each generation, and yet the need and vitality of each generation has been frustrated and complicated by the *status quo* pull of reactionary and ultraconservative spirits.

In thinking about conservatism, we should distinguish between monological and dialogical conservatism. The former is dumb and blind to all other values but its own; the latter keeps itself in a relationship of polarity with the liberal spirit and point of view. Yet each needs the other. Without the liberal position one would not dare to be a conservative; and the liberal is more freely liberal precisely because the conservative helps hold in focus the traditional viewpoint.

Monological conservatism acknowledges no dependence, and contradicts Christ's spirit and teaching. Obedience to its spirit may be our most serious sin because it tempts us to think that we own our institutions, and to exercise proprietorship in matters of the faith. Possessive attitudes toward truth lead to a life of conformity and sterile orthodoxy. Orthodoxy is not our goal! *New life, new meaning, new creaturehood is!* The purpose of obedience to truth is not to graze in the flat lands of orthodoxy, but to climb the sharp, high, narrow ridges of faith in order that we may understand more and more the relevance of the revelation of God to our own age.

How can the dragging tug of a reactionary spirit be overcome and men find in their faith the courage to be and do? A spirit of timidity clutches at us constantly and threatens to choke our creativity, especially when life challenges us by crises growing out of all the "changes and chances of this mortal life." Many examples are to be found in both ancient and modern life.

Moses, in response to God's call to deliver the Jews out of Egypt, reflected the spirit of timidity when he said in his conversation with the Spirit of God, "Who am I that I should go?" or again, "They will not believe me or listen to my voice"; or still again, "O Lord, I am not eloquent but slow of tongue and speech." Likewise, when Jeremiah the Prophet was called, he pleaded, "Ah Lord, behold I do not know how to speak for I am only a youth."

In times of crisis people tend to withdraw timidly. "We do not want anything to happen," says the chorus in T. S. Eliot's *Murder in the Cathedral.* "Seven years we've lived quietly, succeeded in avoiding notice, living and partly living . . . but now a great fear is on us."

The spirit of timidity is afraid of life, afraid of facing its problems. It causes men to use their institutions and forms as places in which to hide from the challenges of new life and truth, and to evade or compromise the great human issues.

The great over-all task of dialogue, therefore, is the restoration of the tension between vitality and form. Our various communities could then become centers for a creative exploration of the relevance of the truth we already know to human problems and for the continued discovery of the reuniting and renewing power of that truth.

We turn now to consider some specific aspects of dialogue's task with reference to the Church.

The Renewal of the Church

The renewal of the Church is inevitably concerned with the forms of its life. As we have seen, forms can stifle or block life, or they can be the instruments of its expression. We have inherited forms that the vitality of past ages produced, and the vitality of our own age may create new ones. Some men venerate the old and fear the new; others are suspicious of the old and try to create anew. Each attitude is dangerous. Old forms may be revived if they are brought again into service of the truth they are meant to serve; and new forms cannot be created by willing to do so, but emerge, instead, out of the dialogue that crisis generates.

The Church and Old Forms

From our past come forms of church life which many regard as fixed once and for all, and adhere to rigidly and inflexibly. We forget that the forms and ways of our life grew out of the specific needs of a particular time and need not be accepted, necessarily, as binding upon each succeeding generation, regardless of its unique needs. And yet, the Church and other institutions fall prey to a formalism that enslaves its creativity, which is defended by the rationalization that we must be faithful to history. This is a misconception of history. Faithfulness to history requires that we accept the heritage of the past but bring it into dialogical tension with the vitality and needs of the present. Our faith in this process rests on the belief that God has his will for the present and the future, just as he had for the past, and that he will participate in and direct the decisions and actions we undertake as we try to meet our contemporary responsibilities.

The Church is always in danger of falling prey to fundamentalist positions which operate in various ways. The most familiar is biblical fundamentalism, which seeks to take the Bible literally as if it were the dictated word of God. Another kind is ecclesiological and ritual fundamentalism, which imposes literally the ecclesiastical law and liturgical practice of one age upon another age and its needs. A third kind of fundamentalism—the one we have been talking about in this chapter—is the fundamentalism of form, which invites adherence to a form that had relevance at a former time but cannot serve present need. When religion is lived in the isolation of a "dated" form, it begins to take on the characteristics of fantasy.

One such form, for example, is the parish system, which was designed during a particular period of history in response to the needs of that time. It is now generally accepted as binding upon congregations as the means for expressing their life. But circumstances have changed and communities are no longer self-contained units with the Church as the center. Mechanization, modern industrial development, increasing communication and transportation, urbanization, have changed our social order so that a local congregation no longer stands at the heart of the life of its people, nor has it the intimate, dynamic relation to the community that it once had. And yet when you ask the average person where his church is, he will identify it as being on a given street corner; and when asked what his church is doing, he will describe the Sunday morning worship, the Christian education program, or its other meetings and activities. He thus reveals that he thinks of his church only in terms of in-church activities. Such a concept creates a cleavage between what goes on in church and what goes on in the world.

A weekend conference conducted for the members of the official board of a local congregation, for example, illustrates how unrelated congregational life may become to the world in which the members live. When it was suggested to these laymen that the meanings emerging from their worship and study together should be applied to their life and work in the world, and that the meanings of their life in the world should be brought into relation with their worship and study, there was bewilderment. One man said, "I intend to keep them separate, they don't belong together." Another said, "When I am in church, I want to forget everything I'm responsible for." Soon the discussion turned to ethics, with most of the men expressing the thought that they justified their church membership by being honest and upright in their business dealings. "It is a simple matter of living by the Golden Rule," said one. But when the question was asked about how possible this was, several men indignantly responded by saying that they had always been honest and had never misrepresented a contract or falsified a report. They further maintained that they saw no reason why there would be any difficulty in being both a good Christian and a good businessman. "I have never done anything wrong," said several. They were then asked why they bothered with church membership or Christian belief since they could live in the world and carry on their business with such complete obedience to the law of God and without need of the mercy and forgiveness of God or of the saving work of Christ.

The attitude and understanding expressed by these businessmen is unfortunately a widespread one and illustrates how when only the form of church life is observed, it nurtures a religion of fantasy that is unrelated to the real world in which men live, and encourages them to create a superficial ethic which they can keep, while preventing them from understanding the true nature of human life and their predicament. Some of these men admitted that the meanings of the words, prayers, hymns, and even of the sacraments in which they regularly participated, were sealed off completely from life and existed only in the fantasy of the "religious life" of their local congregation. Consequently, because the true meanings of their faith were not available to them, their life in the world, by true moral and religious standards, was fantasy, too.

The purpose of dialogue is to keep the meanings of worship and study in tension with the meanings of daily life. Out of this dialogue may come the renewal of the form, in this case the renewal of the congregation. There are congregations whose concept of themselves has been changed radically through dialogue. They no longer think of themselves in terms only of their in-church identity but as an apostolate, as a "sent" people whose reason for existence is out in the world where they live and work honestly and creatively on the frontiers of human life; as a "sent" people whose service of God is not in "church" but on the boards of institutions for the welfare and education of people, in movements concerned with just relations between men, and in the exploration of the responsibilities of Christian churchmen in business, industry, and the life of society. This new concept has the congregation moving out of its worship and study into the world, and back from the world into its worship and study, the members of such a congregation becoming the leaven by means of which God speaks and acts to their generation. The congregation now ceases to be a club of like-minded people protecting their "heritage" out of the past, but the members become engaged in the mission of the Church—and the Church is mission. Such a congregation, by participating in dialogical thinking and living, has regained for itself the distinction of being a center of creative thought and action in its community, a center for experimental living in relation to its community task.

The forms of church life need to be judged constantly against the vitality and need of the times. An incident which occurred in a certain New England church illustrates how necessary for the health of the church is this tension. When a Negro was accepted as a member of the congregation, a lay official of the church and his family withdrew in protest. Other members took alarm and also withdrew. The minister in charge, however, had the courage to stand firm and unmoved by these withdrawals and the threat of others to come. His ecclesiastical superior stood behind him with the statement: "I would expect all of our clergy to have the same courage. What this teaches is how much harder we must work with our children and our adults to bring about in them all the deeper devotion to our Lord so that with hearts overflowing with love for him, they may see in awe who are his, not their coloring nor their race, but Christ's." He added, "There will be no exclusiveness among us, and all who come will find a full welcome." This is commendable, but unfortunately it illustrates how commonly the local units of the Christian Church exist in our communities as if they were exclusive clubs of chosen people, closing themselves off from the Spirit's call to heroic action on the frontline of the battle between the redeeming Christ and the world. The time may not be far distant when the *laos,* the chosen people of God, will have to eliminate from its membership all "club members," whether ordained or unordained, in order that it may be free to get on with the task given to it by its Lord. People who think of the Church as their possession are the enemies of the Church and its mission in the world. The relation is not one of proprietorship, but one in which the members regard themselves as expendable, possessed by the Spirit, and, therefore, members of his Body who would do what he would do in this generation.

Some Thoughts about New Forms

Men who venerate the past and distrust the present and the future reveal by their distrust a distrust of God also. When men really believe in him, they know that whatever the future may bring, they still stand among their fellowmen, trusting in God's unchanging faithfulness. In the assurance of this faith they are able to listen to what he is saying in their own time, a word which he speaks not only through the Church but through the life and thought of the world. If the Church is to communicate with the present generation, it must be a listening Church. A listening Church, in contrast to a monological one, will always be renewed and need not be afraid of change. Instead of being defensive in the face of new human insights and discoveries, the listening Church is able courageously to enter into dialogue with these, fully confident that out of it the truth of God will appear as it always has.

Many church members, however, tend to absolutize what has been believed and formulated in the past, so that their need for perspective is acute. We need, however, to remember that man has been emerging for millions of years and that God has been the source and guide of his appearance. In contrast, the Christian Church is barely two thousand years old; and while its history is venerable and productive, we tend to overestimate and absolutize its developments. But what of the future we ask, for life may go on for another hundred thousand or million years. If Christ is the Truth and the Lord of the new creation, as we profess, what will be the shape of things to come, especially if men have faith in him and courageously participate in dialogue with the meanings of each generation? Are we to stand with our backs to the future, looking steadfastly into the past? Or, are we to stand facing the future, supported by the heritage of the past? Men's understanding of their faith, and of the forms by which they express it, may change so radically that if we were to return thousands of years later we might not recognize them. And yet, the faith would be the same. We need to distinguish between God's revelation of himself *and* our religion, which is simply our response to his revelation. The revelation is complete and changeless, but our understanding and response to it can and should change.

We dare, therefore, to look for change of form and way of life. Present circumstances are producing some interesting variations in the form of the congregation. We have already seen how old forms must change; and although we may not be alert to them, new forms of the congregation are constantly appearing. A Negro woman, for example, was riding on a bus in a southern city. She was seated in the white section and was told to move. For some reason she decided that she would not and thus witnessed to her right to ride where any other person might choose to ride. She was put off the bus and arrested. Thirty or forty other people heard about it and converged on the jail where she was being held, in protest of the unjust arrest. They, too, were jailed, but they found themselves bound together in a fellowship of common cause and devoted not only to it but to one another. Hundreds of others heard about the action; and they also came together in protest and, in turn, were arrested. In the end, almost a thousand people expressed their conviction, accepting suffering in order that justice might be done among men, and the causes of God served. Was this not possibly a new form of the congregation?

A real question for us is: What type of relation, if any, will the traditional congregation have with the new? The new one may be operating under a very primitive theology, one unequal to the task of the congregation. Would it be possible for the old congregation to offer itself to the new in such a way that the historic theology of the Christian Church might be available to guide and sustain the new movement in order that it may find itself and its destiny? Or, will the traditional congregation withhold itself and its resources because the other is so different, so wild and untamed in its manifestation of vitality, and so unrespectable in its method of operation?

And who is to say that in the United Nations and its auxiliary organizations there is not emerging a new form of ministry bringing together the congregation of God's people? Those who now participate in this may not identify it as such, but insofar as what they are doing was, and is, also a ministry of Christ—namely, reconciling man to man— their service is to him; their ministry, his. Here is a form that sprang up in response to the exigencies of our time. Years ago Woodrow Wilson tried to bring a new form into being—the League of Nations. It did not survive, but out of the struggle and dialogue of nations of which the attempted League was a part, the United Nations appeared as a creation of the need and spirit of our age. We cannot create new forms by willing to do so, but have to wait for them to appear out of the dialogue of the crisis. It is required of us that we be alert to these possibilities, open to them, and ready to affirm and participate in them as opportunity comes.

Moving beyond international relations, we all have to face the fact that we are standing on the threshold of an interplanetary age. Already some church people are worried about what the effect will be on present belief if we discover life on the other planets. The fear seems to be that if life exists there, it may have a religion that raises questions about Christianity. People are developing a defensive attitude and getting ready to defend the faith. The faith, if it is all that we profess it to be, is supposed to be our defense. With it we are freed to engage in any truth from anywhere. If God is God, he is the God of all life. Christ is more than Christian. The term "Christian" is only our way of identifying our relation to him. He may be revealed to others in another form, and the response of other beings may be different than ours. Instead of drawing back from the frontiers of life, being opened up by the God-given curiosity, initiative, and inventiveness of men, our religious response should be one of interest, anticipation, and readiness to address in dialogue the meaning of the new with the old, in the expectation that the new will confirm, correct, and amplify the old, and the old will give perspective and structure to the new.

The general task of dialogue is, therefore, one of helping us to accept the idea that the forms of our life may have to be broken because they no longer contain the Spirit which created them; that we ourselves have to be open to the transformation of old forms and the appearance of new ones and to work out what the relation is to be between the old and new; and finally, to give us courage to live on the frontiers of life, accepting the stress of inevitable conflict and possible transformation. Religion needs always to be renewed by the revelations that gave it form in order that it may be in creative relation with the culture in which it lives. Religion and its institution, the Church, must be in constant dialogue with the revelation of God and with the creative enterprises of men. The Church may dare to speak in each age only if it listens both to God and men.

It is not enough to talk about dialogue in the abstract. The principle must be embodied in men. Dialogue calls for dialogists. In fact one of the crying needs in the Church today is for dialogical teachers.

The Dialogical Teacher

There is abundant evidence that the Church, in carrying on its teaching function has put too much faith in the use of words, and used too little the language of relationship. The result is that people have not been helped to understand the meaning of their own experiences or to bring these meanings into relationship with the meaning of the words used in preaching or formal teaching. The teacher ought to be equally responsible for the relationships out of which come the meanings essential to our growing understanding and maturing way of living.

The task we have just described calls for a changed concept of the teacher. And the term "teacher" as used here includes more than the professional teacher, be he educator or minister. All men teach in the sense that, at some time, they have to show others how to do something, or to guide and influence them and, therefore, unconsciously or consciously to educate them. What is being said here, then, about teaching and the teacher has a wide and comprehensive relevance.

The old stereotype of the teacher as one who knows his field and merely tells others about it is unequal to the task of education today. The teacher who abstracts the truth from the life from which it came and to which it belongs cannot be of help to contemporary man who is using every modern means to separate God from his life. Something more than agenda orientation and transmission is needed.

What, then, are the qualities that characterize the dialogical teacher? First, his communication serves the principle of dialogue by whatever methods he uses. He is one who first studies and learns his subject, that is, the part of human knowledge for which he is responsible. It is to be hoped that he will know it not only in itself, but in its relation to other areas of knowledge, and be open to communication with the experts in those other fields.

Second, the dialogical teacher is alert to the meanings that his students bring to the moment of learning. Such a teacher makes himself not only responsible for what he has selected for his students, but also for what they bring him out of their living and learning. He listens to them and tries to imagine what is going on in them. This quality stands in sharp contrast to the arrogance that so often characterizes the behavior of teachers. Dialogical teachers do not view their students with condescension. Neither do they pamper them nor exploit them.

Third, the dialogical teacher endeavors to help his students formulate their questions and meanings as preparation for responding to the information and understandings he is presenting to them. The dialogical teacher realizes that students hear and respond with their own meanings and questions, but because they may not have these meanings and questions available to them, he accepts as part of his task helping them to be aware of themselves and of what they bring. He also recognizes that what goes on between himself and his students is an important part of the curriculum.

Fourth, the dialogical teacher recognizes himself to be a resource person, one who uses his knowledge, wisdom, and skill to help students correlate the meaning of their lives with the meaning of the gospel. Students have to make their own correlations; teachers cannot do it for them. Dialogical teachers do not just give answers to their students. Who, other than the teacher, is better qualified by virtue of what they know and understand to help students ask the great questions and thus prepare them, as otherwise they cannot be prepared, for significant learning? Who is better able to direct the reading and thinking of students? Who, more tragically than teachers, betray their true responsibilities when they do students' thinking for them? Teachers who use their powers to help students find their own powers —and they can do that because they know their students and know where they stand in their studies and preparation —may lecture when it is appropriate to do so as a part of the dialogue in which their students are significant participants.

Fifth, the dialogical teacher strives for a broad understanding of the meaning of dialogue and of its practice. He seeks to create opportunities for students to participate in dialogue with one another, to have the experience under his supervision of communicating that which they are learning, to test their understandings of truth and of one another, to learn skill in choosing the right symbols for expression. He provides opportunity for them to engage in a dialogue with him in which they may be challenged by his knowledge and skill, and, at the same time, know that they are respected by him for what they are able to bring to such an exchange, and, therefore, have their powers of dialogue affirmed and also nurtured.

The dialogical teacher also understands that implicit in dialogue between man and man is a meeting between God and man. He knows that if a person is to speak to God, he must really speak to his neighbor; that if he would love God, he must love his neighbor; and that in loving his neighbor, he will be found of God and loved by him.

Sixth, the dialogical teacher is not defensive about the content he offers. It has been formulated out of life; it is relatable to life. The content and meaning of individual lives need the accumulated content and meaning of generations of human living. The dialogical teacher is able to teach either through the meaning of the subject in relation to meanings of the students, or through the meanings of the students in relation to the meanings of his subject. He will be versatile in his use of methods. If a question needs to be asked, he will use a method that will serve that purpose. If a question has been asked, he will use such methods as will address the answer to the question, whether a lecture, an assigned reading, or some other method. He will not hesitate to speak with authority and with transmissive intent when the educational task indicates, but he will prefer to develop the initiative and the authority of the student when he can. In other words, the dialogical teacher is a versatile teacher.

Seventh, the dialogical teacher believes that each person seeks to find his own special form and task. He is suspicious of conformity, and will not commit acts of piracy on the minds and characters of his students. On the other hand, he offers his students the gift of relationship in order that their personal qualities and capacities may be realized and confirmed. The teacher accepts the independent "otherness" of his students and does not wish to impose upon them his own relation to truth.

Eighth, the dialogical teacher speaks and acts in his capacity as educator and departs from his plan without anxiety because he trusts both the working of the Spirit and the inner workings of his students. In contrast, many teachers do not so trust their pupils or the Spirit. They feel that learning on the part of students is dependent upon the teacher's presence, and that everything that must happen to the students must take place while the teacher is present,

or it will not take place at all. They have not learned that
the teacher is like a farmer who plants the seed and goes
about his other business, leaving the seed to germinate,
interact with the soil, put forth its blade and grow until,
in its own good time, it begins to produce its fruit, only oc-
casional attention being required along the way. Teaching
of this character respects the qualities and capacities of the
learner and his right and responsibility to become what only
he can become.

How does the dialogical teacher accomplish this task?
Through the language of relationship which is an indispensable part of the language of dialogue.* The communication
that results from living together gives us the basic and personal meanings for the words we hear and use. The spirit
of the relationship determines the nature of the communication. The language of relationship, the language of mutual
address and response, of trust and love, must be correlated
with the language of words, for once we have awakened in
another the response of trust, what we teach him in words
will have meaning for him. The religious word "faith," for
example, should at once be the symbol of the meanings the
child can bring out of his experience of basic trust, and also
the symbol of the affirmative meanings that come out of the
experiences of people in their encounters with God. Only
if we are helped to bring the right meaning of trust to our
use of the words "I" and "Thou" will all that the Creed
affirms about what God has done in relation to human need
become available to us.

* See *Man's Need and God's Action* by Reuel L. Howe (Greenwich,
Conn.: Seabury Press, 1953), for a discussion in Chapter V on the language of relationship.

The Ministry of the Church

Another area demanding the Church's consideration is the one concerning the nature of the ministry. When we begin to consider the nature of the ministry we immediately confront the question of orders or form. And here again form needs to be brought into tension with the vitality that produced it in the expectation that reformations and transformations would occur. Concern for orders of the ministry —bishops, presbyters, deacons, and so forth—is one of the chief blocks to Christian unity. The Spirit is calling this generation to an appreciation of, and dependence on, the ministry of all the people and away from a clericalized ministry, one centered in the work of ordained clergy. Today we are thinking increasingly in terms of the ministry of the whole Church, a ministry that includes the work of unordained as well as ordained members. The recovery of this concept of a whole ministry of two kinds raises questions about both. What is the ministry of the layman and of the clergyman?

Changes are already occurring in our thinking about the ministry of laymen. No longer do we regard their church work—ushering, teaching, organizational activities, assisting in services—as their unique ministry. This in-church activity is necessary, to be sure, for the continuation of the liturgical, educational, and organizational life of the Church. In these capacities they assist the ordained minister, into whose care the direction of the church life and program has been put. The layman's true and indispensable responsibility is in the world where he lives, works, and moves. But we are not clear what his ministry should be there. We are not even sure we want to call it a "ministry" because the word has such clericalized meanings attached to it. We do know that the purpose of the Church is to preach the gospel—to proclaim the Good News that in Christ God overcame the two enemies of man, sin and death. But how does the layman do this? One common, and still necessary, understanding of this obligation is that we do it by telling the "story," that is, by reciting the acts of God in Christ. The wonderful story should always be told, but we need to guard against a literalization of it. The "telling," the "preaching," can become formalized so that it no longer conveys the Spirit. It becomes a vain repetition of words and narratives, and the tremendous meaning of the Christ event in history gets jammed into the tiny dimensions of a "Jesus cult" and becomes ridiculous to all but its devotees.

How can the Good News be told so that its liberating power for life is available? It must be told in the same way in which it came. It was made known to us by being incarnate in the life of a man, Jesus of Nazareth, and it can be made known in our generation only by being incarnate in us. The truth that is God, actualized in Jesus, was by him brought into dialogue with human life; and so today the gospel must be proclaimed by being embodied in the lives of those who have received it and brought into dialogue with the lives of men. As Jesus found it necessary to live in the world in order to reveal the Father, so we, too, must live in the world in order to make him known. And while he did talk about the Father, his talk was related to, and given force by, his profound acceptance and use of ordinary human events, meanings, and everyday things. His living made the dialogue between God and man acute and decisive; and it took place not in the synagogue or church but on the streets and roads, in homes and taverns, and finally, on the hill of execution and out of a borrowed tomb. And so our proclamation must be in homes and at parties, on planes and expressways, in business and industry, in schools and laboratories, in political and social movements, at polls and in elective offices, and on the frontiers of human understanding and concern. Most of the time the proclamation must be in the language of relationship: of example, of love and care, of appreciation and criticism, of courage in the face of despair, and by a willingness to take risks for the sake of a cause. Most of the time we have to proclaim by the language of action, and once in a while we may be able to identify, after there is something to identify, him whom we serve and our reason for serving him. The trouble now is that both the clergy and the laity are too anxious about identifying results, about tying labels on the plantings of the Spirit. The concern is often premature since nothing exists that requires an identifying tag. Better would it be first to live, work, and create something that could be labeled later. Furthermore, the Spirit is self-effacing, and God often works anonymously, an insight which should make it possible for us to witness in a more relaxed way.

The layman's ministry, therefore, is in the world, expressed by the way he lives in it and the purposes he serves, embodying in himself a meeting between the Word of God and the word of man. His pulpit or altar, if he has to have one or the other, is his desk or workbench or laboratory or classroom. The key to judging the effectiveness of his ministry is: Who do men see when they come to know one? and,

Does our "meeting" with him add to the meaning and possibilities of life?

The Ministry of the Ordained

The ministry of the ordained member has the ministry of the layman as its context. Pathetic is the condition of a minister who does not realize his need for that context. He is like an arm that has been severed from the body; he is vainly trying to do a part of the work of the body without dependence upon the body. Some ministers preach, for example, as if they could, and should, do it alone, as if the sermon which they prepare and deliver is all-sufficient. How tragic that they do not realize that they need the meanings, thoughts, questions, understandings, interests, and encouragement of their congregation in order to prepare and preach their sermons; and that their sermons, far from being the great production of the occasion, are only a preliminary contribution to the sermons which are formed in each hearer as he responds out of his meanings to the meanings of the preacher. The Church's sermon is the one born in the hearer, and this is the only one taken and delivered in the world. The clergyman's ministry is only auxiliary to the ministry of the whole Church.

The form of the ordained ministry may change when the Church is equally responsive to the Spirit and to the vitality and need of each generation. This is not to say that we should necessarily discard what we have received; but neither should we hold the forms of what we have received so rigidly that it is no longer available to God to make of it what he wills.

The question, then, is how shall we live in this kind of

tension, treasuring what we have and yet expecting what we are to become? The answer is: By keeping the ministry, whatever its present form, focused on its most true and relevant purpose for the time. The present time is one in which men are looking for meaning. Many of them doubt that there is any over-all ultimate meaning and so clutch at any little meaning they can find. Others, believing that there is an enduring meaning, seize upon and settle for partial meanings to which they give their devotion and thus serve idols such as religion, politics, fame, efficiency, success, and so forth. And still others are searching for the pearl of great price, the meaning that connects and completes all meaning. The purpose of the ministry in a generation that is searching for meaning is to meet that search with understanding and response. The meanings of the gospel cannot be imposed on the meanings of each generation like a veneer. As we saw earlier, the relationship between him who was the Good News and his generation was one of dialogue, in which the meanings of man and those of God met. It follows, therefore, that the function of the Church is to be in dialogue with the world; and the function of the pastoral, homiletical, educational, and priestly ministry is to promote and maintain the dialogue between the Word of God and the word of man in order that men may know their own need and possibility, and know and accept what God has given them.

Both the clergy and laity need training that will prepare them to become persons with dialogical understanding and abilities. For a majority of them this would mean a revolution in their present understandings and approaches because of the prevalence among them of the monological attitude and method, which has been ingrained in them both by their life in the Church and the training given them for their ministry.

One frustration experienced by many ministers is that they find themselves separated from their lay people and able to talk with them only about religion and the Church, and that only at the level of program and organization. And laymen speak of the same separation and limited discussion. Most clergy seem not to have been trained to ask their people about their interests, their work, what it means to them, their questions, beliefs, and thoughts. There is limited conversation between clergy and laity because the clergy are not aware that the laity have anything to say that might have meaning in itself or a necessary relation to what they are about to say. Their expectation based on their training is quite the opposite: that their task is to tell people monologically what they should know and believe. A minister's education should increase, rather than decrease, his capacity to communicate with the people to whom he is sent, remembering that communication requires *hearing* as well as speaking. Resources need to be developed which will keep students for the ministry in dialogue with the world from which they came, to which they belong, and will be sent. Clinical training and supervised field work programs are a step in that direction, but they need further development and additional resources need to be found. Practice preaching in seminary, for example, might be addressed not only to one's fellow students and instructors (which is the usual custom) but also to representative laymen invited to the class for the occasion. (If held in the evening, this could easily be arranged.) Lay people are interested in assisting in the training of clergy and will make all kinds of adjustments and sacrifices in order to cooperate. The benefits of lay participation in this kind of training should be obvious. The comments of the teachers and fellow students are always valuable, of course; but of equal, if not more, importance would be the comments of the very people to whom the future minister will be preaching. The comments of the laity could be as valuable to the instructor and the students not preaching as to the student preacher; and the whole experience, including the comments of instructor and students, would be edifying to the lay discussants.

Other resources need to be developed to acquaint the future minister with the world in which he is to serve in order that he may have eyes that see and ears that hear the life that goes on behind the masks that men wear, the questions behind the questions that men ask, and the meanings that they bring out of their life and work to every kind of encounter. Without this kind of training and understanding they cannot "experience the other side" and dialogically proclaim the Good News. Many ministers complain that their preparation for their work was too isolated from, and unrelated to, people and the conditions of their life and work. Even "practical" departments can be too tidy in their presentation of life and the ministry, and mislead future ministers by implicitly suggesting that if they do the right things the right results will be obtained.

Theological education by every adequate means should be theological, but the dialogical task requires that the theology be learned in dialogue. By this we mean: (1) that the theology itself should be brought into dialogue with the questions of our time and be thought out in its idiom; and (2) that the student must learn his theology by participating in that dialogue under the supervision of a theologian-teacher who, presumably, has done the task himself and knows how to guide the students in it rather than trying to do it for them.

It would seem, therefore, that we should change the purpose of our teaching from that of transmitting knowledge about the faith to training men for action in the faith. People should know the gospel, not for the sake of possessing that knowledge, but in order that they may *live* it. The gospel is a saving event that occurs in human relations and is not a body of knowledge for mere verbal transmission. There is a place for knowledge, of course. There is nothing more deplorable and ineffectual than an ignorant minister, whether ordained or unordained; but there is also nothing more sterile than the transmission of information without its incarnation in the personal. Our Lord did not add much to our knowledge of God. He embodied God for us so that we could *know* him, instead of *knowing about* him.

Yet, one of the most incapacitating anxieties of both clergy and laity is the "agenda anxiety," to which we referred earlier. They are so concerned with transmission of content about the Christian faith that they are blind and deaf to its relation to the people themselves, to their meanings, and their questions about human life. They make idols of formulations about the faith and then worship them.

Many clergy are victims of what we may call the "content" illusion. This will continue to be the case as long as centers of learning continue to teach subject matter exclusively and, in so doing, overlook their responsibility for the student and his relation to the world where he will live and to which he is sent. And ministers transmit this preoccupation with content to their people. A man filled with subject matter does not make an adequate minister. An adequate minister is one in whom the meaning of life and the meaning of the gospel are correlated. The "didactic and dogmatic stance," referred to by Richard Niebuhr in his *Advancement of Theological Education,* produces a ministry that is unequal to proclaiming the gospel in our day. When profound questions are being asked in every aspect of life, ministers trained in this way come to resent the indignity of having been turned into subject-matter peddlers instead of having been trained to be ambassadors for Christ.

And the same change is needed in the training of laymen for their ministry. The knowledge about God is no adequate substitute for a readiness on their part to meet and represent God in the encounters and responsibilities of their lives. Preparation for church membership that merely fills individuals with the subject matter of Christian belief, church history, and worship does not begin to prepare modern disciples for their work and witness in the world. They need, instead, help in correlating the meaning of the gospel with the meaning of their lives, and they need help to recognize the questions and meanings in the human situation that call for their word or action as instruments of the Spirit. They need to think through—in terms of their lives, not of religion—what it means to be a member and servant of Christ, and how and where and when they shall serve him in the complexity and concreteness of their living.

A basic attitude of modern man, of church members as well as others, is his desire to rid his everyday existence from any claim of the holy. And he does this by spiritualizing religion—that is, he removes his relation with God into a pure world of the Spirit by denying that relation or by sub-jectivizing it so that it becomes purely immanent, identical with his own inspirations and aspirations. In this way he succeeds in eliminating the uncomfortable dialogue between what he is and what God is. A member of a congregation which was calling a new minister was heard to express the wish that they could find a minister who would concentrate religion in the Sunday program because this man did not want to deal with its complications during the rest of the week. Contemporary man is often interested in religion and the Bible in only abstract terms, and does not want his life to be confronted by the Word. He is afraid of confronta-tion because he cannot stand revelation. Martin Buber has pointed out, "Specifically, modern thought can no longer endure a God who is not confined to man's subjectivity, who is not merely a supreme value."

Unfortunately, much religious teaching confirms us in this separation of God from life by making God a part of the subject matter of life, and religion one of the areas of interest. It is necessary for the teacher to go beyond mere verbal affirmations, assurances, and explanations to an actual awakening of the responses of people to the meaning of life as they experience it in their relations with one another. The hope is that as the dialogue between man and man is re-newed, he will again experience dialogue with God. The Christian's hope is based on the belief that in Christ Jesus dialogue was revealed as a principle of renewal. His Incarna-tion is understood to have been the occurrence of dialogue between man and man, in which God was fully participant; and, as we have seen, that which was begun in the Incarna-tion of the Christ in Jesus is continued now through the incarnation of the Spirit in us. Where we seek one another in honest exchange, we may find ourselves also in communion with God.

The subject matter of true religion is not "religion," but life. Therefore, the teacher needs to talk about life in terms of its ultimate meaning. When these meanings are related to religious symbols, the symbols then come alive and illumine our partial, temporal meanings with the ultimate ones.

The miracles of dialogue are needed in all relationships: individual and social, educational and religious, economic and political, national and international. By dialogue we can let God into our world because in dialogue we open ourselves to one another, and in so doing, we open ourselves to God. When man is open to man and God, miracles have to happen. But they are forged out of everyday events, the happenings between persons: the conflicts, failures, misunderstandings and tragedies of living together, as well as out of the love and acceptance that are both the source and the environment for the working of the miracles of dialogue.

Index